To Wawa with Love

TOM DOUGLAS

JAMES LORIMER & COMPANY LTD., PUBLISHERS
TORONTO

James Lorimer & Company Ltd., Publishers acknowledges the support of the Ontario Arts Council. We acknowledge the financial support of the Government of Canada through the Canada Book Fund for our publishing activities. We acknowledge the support of the Canada Council for the Arts which last year invested $24.3 million in writing and publishing throughout Canada. We acknowledge the Government of Ontario through the Ontario Media Development Corporation's Ontario Book Initiative.

"The Magic of Christmas" and "Where Have All the Soldiers Gone?" were first published in *The Toronto Star*.

"Rocky Takes A Fall" was an award-winner in the City of Ottawa Short Story Contest.

The author acknowledges the financial support of the Ontario Arts Council through its Writers' Reserve initiative.

Cover design: Meghan Collins
Cover images: Photos from the author's collection, the Sault Ste. Marie Museum and the Algoma Ore Division (ADD) Photo Archives, George Burns (www.michiwawa.com), and Johanna Rowe (www.wawahistory.com)

Library and Archives Canada Cataloguing in Publication

Douglas, Tom, 1941-
    To Wawa with love / Tom Douglas.

Also issued in electronic format.
ISBN 978-1-4594-0044-3

    1. Douglas, Tom, 1941- --Childhood and youth. 2. Wawa (Ont.)--Biography. I. Title.

FC3099.W41Z49 2012   971.3'132   C2011-908156-3

James Lorimer & Company Ltd., Publishers
317 Adelaide Street West, Suite 1002
Toronto, ON
M5V 1P9
www.lorimer.ca

Printed and bound in Canada

To my father, for having the guts to stay in the game until he'd been dealt a winning hand.

And to my mother, for backing him all the way.

Contents

Preface

The lung-searing sulphur fumes rolled in on the wind. Those who dared venture out of their clapboard shelters tied handkerchiefs over their mouths to prevent a fit of gagging and choking. Tears streaming down their faces, the hapless victims of this latest gas attack dashed from one spot to another, hurrying to do whatever had to be done.

In the distance could be heard the rumbling of heavy trucks carrying a fiery cargo that, from time to time, spilled down a hillside, searing the grass and turning trees into flaming torches.

As the sun came up, vaporizing the puddles of overnight rain, the sulphurous air turned steamy and dank, inviting another onslaught of blackflies and mosquitoes that left everyone in their murderous path covered in bleeding sores.

If the supply train had managed to get through that morning, chances were that the bread was mouldy and the milk sour from sitting in an unrefrigerated boxcar while the crew strained to remove a rock slide or fallen tree from railway tracks that provided a lifeline from the civilized south.

War zone? It might seem so, but this was a typical day in the small village of Sinterville, in the wilds of Northern

Ontario's iron-ore mining country in the mid- to late-1940s. The sulphur fumes belched out of a smokestack at the nearby sintering plant, where red-hot clinkers were loaded onto huge trucks and then dumped down a hillside that once was covered with trees and grass and wildflowers.

Ironically, our family was sent off to this desolate outpost because my father had spent several years overseas suffering similar hardships—and much worse—on the battlefields of Europe with the Allied invasion forces that landed on the Normandy beaches during the D-Day offensive on June 6, 1944. Not knowing what to do with him upon his return, Dad's former employers had given him, his wife, and two young sons a one-way ticket to the wild and wide-open mining town of Wawa. Sinterville was a dormitory community of some twenty-three ramshackle houses several miles down the road.

I have related here how our family coped with—and eventually triumphed over—this unjust and insensitive five-year posting, my father's war-induced drinking problem, and the deprivation of living in a settlement hacked out of bushland and quagmire, in a series of vignettes that provide an insight into a time and place that has been little documented. I have set down these few memories about that time and place in an effort to prevent it all from slipping away, without a trace, down a sinkhole of history.

Wherever it seemed appropriate, I have told the stories through the eyes and slightly naive observations of my younger self—a precocious child who had been fed a steady diet of gangster movies, westerns, and musical comedies that played at the neighbourhood theatre just around the corner from our apartment building in the early days before my father returned from overseas.

I have changed many of the names to protect the truly

innocent, and time has frayed my memory a little when it comes to exact dates and numbers, but all the stories, with the odd embellishment for dramatic effect, are true. May they serve as a monument to the pioneering spirit of those hardy souls who opened up the northern mining areas of our vast country and as an inspiration to a generation struggling with the more sophisticated challenges of today's world.

Chapter One

OEDIPUS WRECKS A HOMECOMING

M y brother Greg sold out for a pair of white boots. He always did come cheap.

There we were in the clutches of a madman and all Greg could think about was looking good. I'd known he might not understand the danger we were in, but he'd sworn he did. He'd even crossed his heart. Twice. And hoped to die. Which was exactly what I expected to happen now that he'd gone over to the other side.

"Greg runs and hides whenever he sees me coming," the murderer had said to our mother. "Tommy I can understand. He just glares at me. We were told to expect that. He's had you all to himself all the time I was away. But Greg seems terrified of me."

"Take him down to Megginson's and buy him a pair of white boots," our mother said. "He loves to get dressed up. He'll come around if you buy him the boots."

And the little traitor did. He came running back from the shoe store with a big grin on his face. Once inside the apartment, he made a beeline for our mother's bedroom, where he climbed up on the chenille-covered double bed to look at his new boots in the long mirror on the wall. Then he *hugged* the murderer.

I knew then that I was on my own. The other two had been fooled, but I wouldn't fall for any such bribery. Even if it was offered. It was only a matter of time, I figured, before the murderer made his move. I had to be ready for him or all three of us would end up dead in our beds.

I could understand my brother Greg being tricked like that. After all, he was only a little kid while I was, well, almost all grown up. But our mother? Couldn't she see that this killer she'd let into our apartment was just waiting to attack us when we weren't expecting it? Hadn't she learned anything from all those scary movies she'd taken me to?

I'd smelled a rat the moment the man who was supposed to be my father stepped down from the train the day before the white boots caper. My dad was a soldier. This man was wearing a funny brown suit with coloured ribbons on his chest, but anybody could dress up like that. If he was really a soldier, where was his rifle? And why wasn't there a big brass band to meet him like there was for the other dads when they'd come home from the war a long time ago? How come we were the only people at the train station? Why wasn't somebody there to give him a medal? Where were all the people with flags and signs and those little rolls of coloured paper that you threw around while everybody shouted, "Welcome home, Mel"?

I kept asking those questions and tugging at the hem of my mother's best dress, but all she wanted to do was throw her arms around this…this stranger…and kiss him for the longest time and then cry. If she was really happy to see him, why was she crying? Was she keeping something from me? She'd never done that before.

He'd made his first mistake when he grabbed me up in his arms and tried to kiss me. This man definitely wasn't my father. He smelled like Uncle Harry the time he came to our apartment dressed like Santa Claus and read Greg and me a story, just before he fell into the Christmas tree. My dad hadn't smelled like that when he'd kissed me goodbye before going off to war. I was sure I would have remembered.

And this man wasn't anything like my dad when you took a really close look at him. Mother used to tell us that our daddy smiled with his eyes. She'd say that again and again whenever we looked at the photo albums she kept by her bed. We used to do that a lot. Look at old photos, I mean. But it wasn't the happiest of times. Mother always ended up hugging the album and crying. Especially after she got a letter telling her our dad wouldn't be coming home yet because he had to help "demob" the other soldiers. I didn't know what "demob" meant, but it sounded pretty fishy to me.

This man didn't smile with his eyes. His eyes were narrow and mean looking. You got the feeling he'd seen a lot of horrible things. I was puzzled for a while, but then I remembered. They were like the eyes of the murderer in one of the movies we'd seen, where a creepy guy came to live with an English family in their apartment and ended up killing them all in their beds.

Somehow this man, who was trying to make us believe he was our father, must've murdered our real father. Then he'd found out where we lived and had come to kill us all in our beds the first chance he got.

I'd decided not to let him know I was on to him because he might pull a knife or gun and rub us all out before we knew what hit us. It was better to keep my kisser shut and wait for the right moment to get the drop on him. That's what my hero Bogie and all the other movie tough guys did.

After we'd come home from the train station, the murderer must have slipped something into the champagne my mother had taken down from the closet shelf and put in the refrigerator earlier that day. He tried to get my brother and me to try some of it, but I'd warned Greg that this man was out to kill us, so we didn't drink any. Well, I pretended to and Greg used up his one trick by saying, "I don't wanna!" and breaking into tears.

Greg got real ginger ale instead, but I decided not to drink anything because I had to keep my mind clear. I tried to warn our mother about her doctored drink by staring hard at her glass and shaking my head a little when she looked at me, but she didn't get it. She drank the whole thing in one swallow and did the same thing again when the murderer refilled her glass and said, "Cheers, baby." Before long she started giggling.

I knew it! Whatever the murderer had put in my mother's drink was starting to work. Now I really had to be careful. I had to do the thinking for all of us or we'd really be in trouble.

As I watched the champagne disappearing glass after glass, I thought about my real father and how this murderer had killed him. My eyes got hot and the tears started to come, but when they asked me about it, I made up a story I knew they'd buy—that I'd been reading too many comic books.

I had to be careful not to let the killer know I'd figured out his plans. I was sure that's how my real dad would have wanted me to handle it.

When the champagne bottle was empty, the murderer gave our mother a funny look, like he was trying to put her under his spell. It worked. She grinned and nodded and told

Greg and me it was time for bed.

I knew for certain then that she'd been drugged, because it wasn't even dark out yet. The next clue was that she told us we could skip our baths just this once. Our mother would never act that way unless someone was controlling her mind. To her, godliness was next to cleanliness.. That's what our next door neighbour used to say anyway. And things got worse. As soon as we were tucked into bed, our mother and the murderer went into her bedroom. And shut the door.

It took me a couple of minutes to get Greg to do what needed to be done. Since I'd already told him the man in the other room was a mad-dog killer, he wasn't exactly thrilled by the idea of knocking on the door and asking if he could sleep in the big bed like we both used to do. I tried to make him believe that our mother wouldn't let anything happen to him, and when he still wouldn't go I started reminding him about all the ghosts and goblins we had under our beds.

That did it. He began howling like he always did, ran out of the room, and started banging on our mother's bedroom door, his thumb stuck in his mouth and his teddy bear under his arm. Before you knew it, the door opened, a hairy arm reached out and Greg and teddy disappeared.

The way I had it figured, the murderer would let things settle down a bit and then begin by killing Greg. I had it all planned that when the screaming started I'd run into our mother's bedroom, rescue her, and be out of there and at the police station before Greg had breathed his last gasp.

But things didn't go exactly as planned. The screaming never did start, and I must have drifted off to sleep. When I woke up the next morning, Greg was sound asleep in the other bed, and I could smell bacon frying. Well, at least my little trick had delayed things.

It was after breakfast when our mother suggested the trip

to the shoe store. While she and I were alone, I tried to bring up the subject about the terrible danger we were in, but she kept humming little tunes and smiling for no reason at all. Before I knew it, Greg was back with his new boots, and I'd lost my chance to say anything.

However, I'd come up with another plan while they were away—one that always worked in the movies. You had to convince the guilty party that if anything happened to you, the police would be sent evidence of the crime. All I had to do was wait for the right moment.

My chance came once our mother had finished calming Greg down, after he'd started jumping on the bed in his new boots and fell off, bumping his head. He was always bumping his head, or getting it bumped for him.

"Oh, by the way," I said in my best private eye voice, "I wrote a letter today and gave it to one of my friends."

The murderer frowned at me, but I pretended not to notice. Our mother was peeling apples for a pie, and Greg was walking around in circles, looking at his new boots.

I had to wait a few minutes because Greg wasn't watching where he was going and bumped into the open pantry door. It took even longer to get him to stop crying this time.

"As I was saying," I began again, "my friend, who shall remain nameless, has the letter I wrote. If anything happens to any of us, that letter goes straight to the police."

The murderer and my mother exchanged glances. Couldn't she see the look of guilt that was written all over his face?

"Tommy has quite an imagination," the murderer said, staring at me again. "Do you think we should have him checked out by a…"

"Of course he has a vivid imagination," my mother broke in. "He's seen every movie that's played in this town for the past three years. And he reads everything he can get his hands on. I started teaching him when he was three."

And that was the end of that.

But every once in a while I'd catch the murderer frowning at me, and I knew he was starting to catch on that I had him pegged.

Days went by and nothing out of the ordinary happened, unless you count the fact that our mother seemed to be enjoying the new arrangements. I tried to tell Aunt Betty about the whole thing when she came to visit, but she just smiled and patted me on the head and helped herself to another chocolate.

I continued to keep my guard up, carefully watching the man I now thought of as "The Murderer Among Us"—a title I'd picked up at our grandparents' place from a *True Crime* magazine Grandma Hazel kept on her night table, where she thought it was safe from prying eyes.

The day came, finally, when it looked like the killer was ready to make his move. He came home from a job interview looking as though he'd just been told he had to go back to war again. When he said we'd all be moving to some place that sounded like "Splinterville," the hair on the back of my neck started to rise.

But we got all excited when our mother greeted this news with the suggestion that we might as well move to the North Pole. Greg and I ran outside to tell all our friends we were going to live with Santa, but before we could find anybody we got called home for a family powwow.

When it was explained to us that we were actually moving to a place called Sinterville, many miles north of Sault Ste. Marie on the Algoma Central Railway line, my alarm system let off more bells and whistles than the scratchy Spike Jones record I used to play over and over again—until it got mysteriously broken.

The murderer was planning the old throw-them-off-the-train trick. Thank goodness I'd seen so many gangster films. And because I had, I'd be ready the first time the train pulled into a station while everyone else was asleep. I'd gently wake up our mother, put my hand over Greg's mouth to keep him quiet, and lead us all off the train and into the safe hands of the police. They'd finally get their man, thanks to me, and I'd probably have to go to the mayor's office to accept a medal or something. Maybe somebody would even make a movie about the whole thing.

I could hardly wait for the trip to begin.

Chapter Two

REPRIEVE FOR AN INNOCENT MAN

The time leading up to our move went by quickly. Greg and I had been given the job of going through our toybox to choose what we could take with us and what we had to give away to friends. But I hadn't forgotten that the murderer had plans for us, so I had to be careful what I said or did.

I avoided him whenever I could because I didn't want him to know that I had figured out what he was up to. And I tried to keep Greg away from him as much as possible because the little rat couldn't keep a secret. I didn't want him to blurt out that we knew the man was an imposter who was just waiting for his chance to wipe us all out.

Then my mother spoiled the whole thing.

I was in my bedroom reading a *NYOKA The Jungle Girl* comic book. Charles Atlas was on the back page, bragging about how he used to be a ninety-eight-pound weakling who let bullies push him around? Then he discovered Dynamic Tension, whatever that was, and he had turned into a muscleman who could beat up anybody—including that bully who had kicked sand in his face. While I was trying to figure out if there was a way I could get turned into a muscleman in a hurry, there was a knock on my bedroom door.

"Who is it?" I asked, and then realized the only person it could be was my mother. Brother Greg and the man who claimed he was our father had gone out for an ice cream cone. I had said I didn't want one, even though I really did. Greg would probably come back home with the stuff all over his face and I'd be jealous, but I figured I had to spend as little time with the murderer as possible until the right moment came along.

My mother came into the room and I moved over on the bed she could sit down. She had that look on her face that told me she had something serious to say. Like the time she told me she would always love me very much but we would soon have another person coming to live with us. How she knew so far ahead that the stork would be dumping a baby brother on us was something I still hadn't figured out. Was it about to happen again? If so, I hoped I got a vote this time.

But it was even worse than that. "Tommy, I know you've been having a hard time getting used to having your dad back home after he's been away for so long," she said, "but we're a family again, and both your dad and I want you to be happy about it."

I didn't say anything. How could I make her see that this wasn't the same man that had gone away to war? How could I get her to realize the danger we were all in?

She tried again. "You've been giving your dad a lot of dirty looks, and you won't talk to him. That really hurts his feelings. He's had a very bad time of it the last few years and he needs all of us to be nice to him."

I couldn't keep it inside me anymore. I threw down the comic book and turned to face my mother. "He's not our dad! Can't you see he's a fake? He doesn't look like our dad. He doesn't smell like our dad. And he doesn't talk like our dad."

This seemed to shock my mother. She took a deep breath, and her forehead got kind of wrinkly. But I could understand that. It must have been hard for her to realize she'd been fooled by the man she thought was her husband. Then she did the one thing I always hated to see her do. She started to cry. Not the way I cried when I was trying to get my own way. She was real quiet about it, but tiny tears started running down her cheeks.

"Your dad has been away at war," she said softly, wiping away one of the tears. "He saw some terrible things happen, and he didn't know from one day to the next if he would ever get back home. And now that he's back, he needs to know that we love him and that we're a happy family once again. I know it's hard to get used to having someone else around after all this time, but you have to try." She paused for a moment and then added, "We all have to try."

I figured this was my chance to ask the question that had been bothering me for a long time: "If the war was so bad, why did he go in the first place? Eddy Lefave's father didn't go. Gino Rinaldi's father didn't go. Judy Bennett's father didn't go. Why did our dad have to go and leave us here all alone? Gino's father takes the whole family to the beach every Sunday. And Judy's father took her to the circus when it was here. All we ever got to do was go to those crummy movies all the time."

I knew when I said it that my remark about the movies would hurt my mother's feelings, and I was sorry as soon as the words came out of my mouth. I loved the movies and I loved going to them with my mother—even if Greg whined through most of them, wanting to go home. I don't know why I said what I said. Sometimes I wish I could keep my big trap shut, just like John Wayne told that guy in the cowboy movie to do a few weeks ago before my dad came home—I mean, before the murderer came to live with us.

My mother was quiet for a while. I hated that almost as much as I hated hearing her cry. Finally, she sighed and started talking again.

"You remember when Aunt Betty and I took you and Greg and your cousin Randy to Bellevue Park on the bus," she said. "You were having a nice time playing catch with some of the other kids and then one of the bigger boys came over and took your ball away and wouldn't give it back?"

I nodded. I remembered how proud I'd felt when I and a couple of other kids I was playing with finally went over to the bigger kid and made him give the ball back by telling him we'd beat him up if he didn't. I don't think he believed us at first. Heck, even I didn't believe us—and I was scared about what would happen next. It had been my new pal Gary McDonald's idea, and he didn't seem scared at all. He was just as big as the other kid, and when Gary started towards him, the other kid threw the ball at us and ran away.

"You remember I explained to you that that boy was a bully, and if you stand up to a bully he'll back down every time?" my mother continued. "Well, there are a lot of bullies in the world. One of them was called Hitler. He had a big gang of bullies that did whatever he told them to do. Your dad and a lot of other brave people decided to stand up to him. It took a long time, but they finally got rid of him."

"But why did they have to go so far away to do it?" I asked. "And why didn't those other kids' fathers go too?"

My mother smiled a little and then explained that my dad and the other soldiers had to go where the bully lived to get back all the stuff he and his gang had taken from people.

"And Eddy Lefave's father wanted to help but he has a bad heart so they wouldn't let him go. I can't explain why the others didn't go. I guess they had their reasons. But your dad went because he knew that if he didn't stand up to that bully, he would some day come here and take everything we have away from us."

That made sense, but it didn't explain why the man who said he was our dad wasn't the way I remembered him when he went away. I decided to put all my cards on the table—another John Wayne expression—and so I asked my mother about it.

"Your dad saw his best friend killed in the war," she said, another tear starting down her face. "It wasn't like the movies, where a man gets shot and then you see him in another movie a few months later. They were using real weapons, and it was horrible to see what happened to Murray Kirby. That was your dad's friend's name. He died and, just like your pet goldfish, that was the end of him. He's never coming back. We talked about that when Monstro died, remember?" (I had called my goldfish "Monstro" after the whale in the Disney movie *Pinocchio*.)

"Your dad saw lots of people, good and bad, killed in the war. And he didn't know if one of those bullets that were flying around would kill him too. It was a terrible time for him, and it changed him a lot. He picked up some bad habits that he's trying to break, but he's still your dad, and he needs you to love him, even if he doesn't seem like the man who went away."

At this point, my mother took a Kleenex from the sleeve of her sweater and blew her nose. I don't know why, but I got the feeling that a lot of the things she was saying to me she was also saying to herself. I got to thinking that maybe I had been wrong all this time. My mother, as far as I knew, had never lied to me. And she was a really smart person. So if she said this man was my dad but that he had changed a lot, I figured I'd better go along with that. I decided that I had to help my mother deal with the things that were bothering her. And I could start by being nicer to my dad because it sounded like he needed my help too. It wasn't going to be easy, but I'd give it my best shot, as John Wayne would say.

Just then Greg and my dad returned from the store, and they had brought back a pint of Neapolitan ice cream with them. It was my favourite—vanilla and chocolate and strawberry all in one box. I liked it so much that I had learned how to spell it and pronounce it so that I could spot it in the cooler or ask for it whenever my mother sent me to the store to get some for dessert.

"Hey, Tommy," my dad said after my mother had smiled at him and nodded her head for some reason. "There's a Laurel and Hardy movie playing at the Princess Theatre. How about you and me going to see it one of these days? Just the two of us. Greg can stay home with your mother."

That settled it. A murderer wouldn't enjoy a Laurel and Hardy movie. This had to be my dad. I even remembered that smile he was smiling, just like before he went away. And my mother was right. He did smile with his eyes.

Maybe it wouldn't be so hard living with another person around after all.

Chapter Three

SALUTE TO SINTERVILLE

Having his sons think of him as an evil imposter, intent on mass murder, must have been close to the final straw for my father.

He'd given up a promising position in the executive suite of the local steel mill to enlist in the army, instead of waiting to be drafted. He'd been shipped overseas and saw his best buddy, Murray Kirby, blown to smithereens on the D-Day beaches. After a year of dodging shells, machine gun fire, and sniper bullets from Normandy to Belgium to the Reichswald, he'd had a new kind of bombshell dropped on him when the fighting stopped.

Before the war, he'd been personal assistant to the general manager of the steel plant because he could type and take shorthand. These skills were soon discovered when he joined the army, and he'd become the Radar O'Reilly of his unit—typing up daily routine orders and handling all the other administrative duties that befell an orderly room sergeant with the 19th Field Regiment of the Royal Canadian Artillery. It might sound like a cushy job, but the 19th was in the thick of the action from D-Day onward. Dad saw more than his share of carnage on a number of battlefronts—horror stories that he would only hint at after the war, and then only after he'd downed more than a few shots of whiskey in a futile attempt to blot out the memories.

When the war ended and everyone was looking forward to all the good things peace would bring, Dad's commanding officer informed him that his services were still needed to do all the necessary paperwork—the process that was required to "get the boys home." Eight long months after the boys had gone home to a hero's welcome, my father stepped off the train in Sault Ste. Marie into the sub-zero temperatures of a January afternoon in 1946.

The general indifference that greeted my father's home-coming hurt him deeply, but he did his best to shrug it off as simply another of the disappointments and indignities a soldier had to learn to accept. It was only when he'd had those shots of whiskey that his bitterness bubbled to the surface. And those belts of rotgut occurred with dismaying regularity. He'd gone into the military a teetotaler, but army life and the atrocities he'd witnessed on the field of battle had driven him to the bottle when hostilities ceased—an emotional wreck who managed to hold on to his sanity by anesthetizing himself with booze whenever the heebie-jeebies hit.

His saving grace was that despite all the horrors of war he'd witnessed, he'd managed to keep his wry, self-deprecating sense of humour. On the rare occasions he was persuaded to tell a few war stories, he invariably drew them from the funnier memories tucked away in his knapsack.

There was the time in Belgium, for instance, when he was sent up a dirt road to alert a nearby artillery battery that had a conked-out field radio and couldn't hear the frantic calls that they were shelling a house where Allied wounded had taken refuge in the basement. Puffballs of dirt kept flying up all around him but in the noise of battle he couldn't hear his mates shouting and figured the soil was being lifted off the dry ground by heavy raindrops. Only when he reached his destination did he learn that the plumes of dust were caused by machine gun bullets being fired at him from a Nazi gun emplacement in the upper part of the shelled building.

He never failed to get a laugh when he related how one of his buddies chug-a-lugged half a jug of what he thought was brandy confiscated from a German farmer, only to learn that he'd treated himself to a quart of castor oil.

A perennial favourite was the one about the time Dad had sung some crude lyrics to a Scottish ballad in an English beer hall and discovered—too late—that the drinker standing next to him at the bar was a six-and-a-half foot, sentimental, and homesick Scottish soldier. "It's nae 'Nelly Put Yer Belly Next to Mine and Wiggle Yer Bum,'" said the Scot. "It's 'You've Never Smelt the Tangle of The Isles.' Do you get that, boyo?"

My father, dangling with his feet six inches off the floor at the end of the enraged Highlander's extended tree trunk of an arm, allowed as how he now knew the real lyrics and would forever after sing them properly. He lied, of course. Nellie wiggled her bum in song every time Dad and his wartime cronies got together around the piano in our parlour, right up until the year he died.

These and other stories were fun to hear. But whenever Dad's drinking took him past the mellow stage into the darker recesses of self-pity and acrimony, he would mutter a well-worn litany of remembered slights.

There was the long, cold train ride home to Sault Ste. Marie after the troop ship docked in Halifax. Whether real or imagined, he remembered the civilian passengers on the train looking askance at this walking anachronism who was wearing a uniform that should have been stored away months before.

There was the insult endured at a stopover along the way. My father and some of his fellow non-commissioned officers had been told to take their meals in the officers' mess because the sergeants' mess was closed for repairs. A beefy officer, whose meagre collection of chest ribbons attested to a war spent entirely on the home front, upbraided the mess steward for not being able to supply him with a second piece of pie, then looked down his puffy red nose at the visiting NCOs and sniffed, "There used to be seconds before this riffraff arrived." Dad always maintained that his mates had to restrain him from hitting the officer—and getting himself court-martialled—but it was so out of character that we relegated that part of the tale to the second-guessing practised by war veterans, jilted lovers, and weekend fishermen.

The theft of his kit bag, containing the souvenirs, personal belongings, and small treasures that represented all his worldly goods from the war years, was another sore spot for Dad. Presumably it was lifted by a light-fingered railroad employee who'd slipped into an unguarded baggage car somewhere along the thousands of miles of railroad track that were taking Dad back to kith and kin.

But the final insult, the blow that had been delivered after he'd come home safely from war-torn Europe, was the one that caused the most pain.

The executives of Sault Ste. Marie's Algoma Steel Corporation—most of whom had shed crocodile tears at having to stay behind to run the plant—had promised all the brave lads who'd enlisted that there would be a job waiting for them when they returned from overseas. But Dad hadn't noticed that the operative article was "*a*" job.

"Good to have you back, Mel, and of course we have a job for you!" they said when he reported for work, optimistic about the future and eager to start rebuilding his life. "What's that? You want your old job back? But that's impossible. Carson's been handling things ever so well since you, uh, since you left us, and it wouldn't be fair to make him give it up after all these years, now would it?"

Carson, who'd been climbing the corporate ladder and making powerful friends while Dad was climbing down the netting into a landing craft to face a ruthless enemy, eventually made it all the way to executive vice-president. Dad was made timekeeper at the Helen Mine, the company's iron ore property in the hinterlands near Wawa on the shores of Lake Superior—a job that was about ten rungs lower than the position he had left to fight for his country.

And that's how my family ended up in Sinterville, a collection of twenty-three glorified shacks huddled up against an outcropping of the Precambrian Shield, about 150 miles north of Sault Ste. Marie on the Algoma Central Railway line. It was the cheapest housing in the Wawa area, and the money hadn't exactly been rolling in during the previous three years.

Whenever I mention the name Sinterville, people's faces take on a blank stare and they mutter, "Centreville? That sounds nice. Kind of homey." I usually agree, having long since given up trying to explain that the place got its name from the sintering plant that belched sulphur fumes at us when the wind blew from the wrong direction.

"Sintering" was a procedure for extracting iron ore from rock. The material arrived by tram bucket from the Helen Mine near Wawa, a few miles away through impenetrable bush and swampland.

The buckets dumped the iron-laden rock into crushing machines that pulverized it—along with the occasional plant worker who happened to fall into the machinery—and the small particles of gravel this produced were dumped into a vat of chemicals.

By some magical process called "sink-float" that I never understood, the rock sank to the bottom of the vat and the iron floated to the top, where it was skimmed off. This sludge was roasted in gigantic ovens to liquefy the iron, which was then poured into moulds to form ingots when it cooled.

The ingots were shipped to the steel mill in Sault Ste. Marie by the same railroad that had delivered a disillusioned soldier, his heartsick wife, and two kids to this Northern Ontario gulag.

The residue from the huge ovens, called slag, was transported to large slagheaps by gigantic vehicles referred to as Euclids—which resembled oversized dump trucks.

The most popular kid in the area was the one whose father, a Euclid mechanic, patched up a discarded inner tube from one of those monsters and let us all float on it when we went swimming at Wawa Lake.

The slagheaps towered into the sky and covered acres of the scrubland surrounding the sintering plant. On the night shift, the slag embers, just pulled from the furnace, would glow brightly, and you could sit on a hill near the dump and watch the Euclids deliver their fiery cargo. I've never seen a live volcano in action, but I would imagine the molten lava looks a lot like the newly dumped slag that tumbled down the side of one of those heaps.

It was the slag dumping that finally spelled the end of Sinterville. The plant ran out of space to dump its molten waste, and so a corporate directive was issued to move the twenty-three houses out of Sinterville down the dirt road to Wawa, about five miles away. If a house was too fragile to move, it was bulldozed flat and its inhabitants were left to find other accommodation wherever they could. The old boys who ran the mine didn't give a fig whether you had a roof over your head, as long as the work got done.

We left Wawa ahead of the Great Sinterville Exodus and, except for an overnight stop years later, I've never been back, so I don't know if there's even a marker to commemorate the one-time existence of the tiny collection of huts known as Sinterville.

I hope there is.

Chapter Four

WILD GOOSE CHASE

" Wawa" is the Ojibway word for "wild goose"—which is what my parents probably figured the fickle finger of fate had inflicted upon them by banishing them to the relative obscurity of a rough-and-tumble outpost in Northern Ontario after all they had been through during the war years.

But for a young city kid suddenly dropped into the midst of a wide-open, wooden-sidewalked, mud wallow of a mining town, Wawa offered a delicious peek at the kind of depravity the movies only hinted at.

The streets weren't paved with gold, but they were littered with drunken miners who always had a quarter to spare for an enterprising youngster ready to run down the street and fetch them a ham and cheese sandwich from the local snack bar or a pack of cigarettes from a nearby confectionery store.

Did I notice your eyebrows shoot up when I mentioned that kids were sent to buy cigarettes for the miners too drunk or too preoccupied at one of the town's perpetual floating poker games to go themselves?

In the Wawa of the late 1940s, there was no such thing as

political correctness. If I could have taught my dog Tuffy to carry loose change and ask for the smokes by name, somebody would have sold them to him—along with anything else he had a fancy for.

That's why, after only a couple of days' stay at Perkovich's Hotel, I was greatly disappointed to learn that the Douglas family wouldn't be living there but would be taking up residence in Sinterville. If Wawa, with its wild and wanton ways, was the 1940s Tombstone we used to see in all those western movies, Sinterville was Buzzard Flats.

Sinterville's idea of a good time was to head down to Durrell's Gully come noon and watch the steam train negotiate the high trestle bridge over the Magpie River. At night, we'd all stare up at the northern lights and comment on how they got prettier with every sighting.

Not that it was all that bad for the average youngster. Within a stone's throw of your house, you could pick wild hazelnuts, blueberries, sugarplums, raspberries, strawberries, and chokecherries. And, yes, I learned the hard way that it was only a stone's throw from my house. There's a special subsection of Murphy's Law for kids that says, "Any stone thrown randomly will always break a window."

There were death-defying hills to toboggan down in winter. And there were great stands of timber where you could while away those lazy summer days doing all sorts of risky things, far from the watchful eyes of a worried mother or a meddlesome little brother.

But my dad wasn't the only one to come out of World War II with an addiction. He'd fallen into the clutches of the demon rum. I was hooked on Hollywood. And I needed a steady supply of quarters to keep feeding my habit. The quarters I hoped to earn running errands for miners were my entry fee to Saturday afternoons at the movies. Well, movie, actually. They sent two up each week by train from Sault Ste. Marie. Usually there was a western for the kids and a romantic comedy or thriller for the adults on Saturday night—if the Lions Club hall, where the films were shown, hadn't been left in ruins by the afternoon crowd of rampaging youngsters.

While my father had been away at war, Mom had whiled away the long, lonely hours between shifts as a welder at the steel plant by taking in every film that played at Sault Ste. Marie's three movie houses.

Since youngsters, and babes in arms, were admitted free when accompanied by an adult, dragging us along instead of paying a babysitter meant money saved. And, having no one else to do a post-movie critique with, my mother would chat away to me about the relative merits of John Hodiak and Ray Milland, or Virginia Mayo and Joan Bennett.

By the time I was four years old, I was considered our neighbourhood's equivalent of Louella Parsons, the Hollywood film critic of that era. I've been told that box office receipts at the nearby Princess Theatre rose or fell depending on what one opinionated little kid thought of their double feature.

Imagine my shock then, when the reunited family was hustled off to Wawa, where I learned they showed only one movie a week for kids, charging twenty-five cents for the privilege.

A new-found friend, much more worldly than I, assured me that quarters were easy to come by. The town was full of miners every Friday night, pockets bulging and gullets parched. Once the good time gals and the dispensers of rotgut were through with them, there were still crumbs to be had as they raced each other to see who could go broke the fastest.

I never got a chance to test his theory. Within days, we

were ensconced in our Sinterville shanty, and although Wawa was a mere five miles or so and a free bus ride away, no son of my mother's, to paraphrase her one and only discussion on the matter, was going to roll drunks in the streets of Wawa and that was that.

Which left me with what seemed like an insurmountable problem.

Twenty-five cents was a king's ransom in those days, and the only thing I had to ransom was a whiny little brother. I ran that one up the flagpole once and learned, much to my disgust, that as the older brother I would be held responsible for anything that happened to the little suck.

There was nothing left but to *earn* the price of admission. So I did—discovering very quickly there were 101 ways to come up with twenty-five big ones every week if you really had to.

The saggy old couch in our living room was always good for a few wayward pennies and nickels after a weekend party at our house. But since such booty was considered communal property, I had to share anything I dredged up from under the cushions with brother Greg and later, after another surprise visit by the stork, brother Norm.

There were all those wild berries to pick, but we usually ate as many as we gathered. And a couple of hours picking under a hot sun gave us such a powerful thirst we'd sell our berries to the canny Sinterville housewives at a fraction of their worth and blow most of the profits at the lemonade stand set up down the street by Mary Jane Chrobak. That was her way of earning *her* movie money, and it didn't dawn on me until much later that we were doing all the work, and she was reaping the benefits.

Dew worm picking was another money maker, but it was a back-breaking chore scouring neighbourhood lawns with a flashlight late at night for the slimy critters. The going rate at the bait stores was four worms for a cent, so this was a job reserved for a desperate Friday night when you hadn't quite made enough throughout the week to earn your place on a hard bench in the Lions Club hall on Saturday afternoon.

There was the occasional penny to be made by finding a discarded beer bottle in a ditch or alleyway. Howard McCabe, Sinterville's teenage precursor of Donald Trump, would take the bottles off your hands and save them up until he had ten or twelve cases, then ship them by train to the brewery in Sault Ste. Marie for a refund of two cents a bottle. The brewery was so happy to get them because of the shortage of glass bottles as a result of the war, they even paid the freight charges.

In winter, you could make a dime pitching in to shovel off the small rink where the miners and the millworkers battled each weekend to see who could break the most bones or remove the most teeth. But nobody at that time would have considered paying their own kids to shovel the walk, and since every household had at least one able-bodied youngster as slave labour, there was no money to be made there.

I thought I'd hit the motherlode one Saturday after taking in a western about a gunman who turns preacher. We had an old shed behind our house, and all it took was one nail and two pieces of wood to turn it into a cross-bearing church.

Jimmy Hall "borrowed" some hymnals from the real house of worship where his father worked as the janitor, an upended orange crate draped with my mother's good tablecloth served as an altar, and a couple of planks resting on chunks of firewood provided pews as comfortable as any I'd ever fidgeted on.

An old cowbell called the neighbourhood to worship and the pre-publicity (Jimmy told his three mouthy sisters) must

have worked because kids came running from far
to hear Reverend Thomas spread the good word.
so ecumenical in our service that we even held cor_____
with me telling professed bedwetter Madeline Hall to "go
and pee no more."

The best part was when the service was over, and the
congregation had dispersed. The take was seventy-six cents.
What an easy way to make a living!

But it was a short-lived career. I ended up being defrocked
faster than a garter snake shedding its skin. Jimmy Hall was
caught returning the hymnals, and he ratted on our little
set-up when the choir director kept insisting she'd caught
him red-handed *stealing* the books. Imagine being threatened with eternal damnation for returning something. It
doesn't seem fair somehow.

Anyway, my parents laid down the law. I was to return
every last cent of the money I'd collected, even if it had
been given voluntarily. And Madeline Hall swore she'd put
in seventeen cents, when I'm positive she was the one who'd
thrown a big red button into the collection plate.

Despite suffering reverses such as this, I still managed to
come up with twenty-five cents every Saturday for as long as
we lived in the Great White North.

I got so used to the deprivation of there being only a
single showing of one movie a week, I lost all sense of time
and place the summer I was allowed to visit my paternal
grandparents in Sault Ste. Marie.

For starters, the neighbourhood theatre in the Sault
only charged eleven cents admission and for that you got
previews, a cartoon, and two full-length features—which
repeated all day long and well into the evening. For twenty-
five cents I could dine like a king on popcorn and a box of
candy as well.

I remember my first day in the big city, heading to the movies in time for the start of the show at 11 a.m. Then it's all a blur until about the fourth or fifth time the opening credits of a Rocky Lane western were rolling, and I felt a hand on my right arm.

Looking up bleary-eyed into the flashlight of a uniformed usher, I stammered out a weak "yes" when he asked me if I was Tommy Douglas.

"Well your grandmother phoned and says you should get the hell home!" was his terse reply as he snapped off his flashlight and strutted back up the aisle.

As I raced home along the dimly lit evening streets of the city, I could hardly wait for this vacation to end so I could tell Bruce McDermid and Gerry Johnson back home in Sinterville all about the night I was thrown out of the Orpheum Theatre in Sault Ste. Marie.

Chapter Five

LEST WE FORGET

The first time it happened, I thought a banshee from hell had landed on my bedroom windowsill and was screeching to her packmates that they'd finally tracked me down.

Well, what would you expect from a young kid with a vivid imagination who'd just been wakened from a sound sleep by the strangest racket imaginable?

This was my introduction to a ritual that from then on marked an annual event most people consider a solemn occasion—the November 11 honouring of those who died in the service of their country.

The noise by which I had been so rudely awakened was the squawk of a set of bagpipes on our lawn. The piper, who'd served in the British Army during World War II, had obviously lubricated more than his chanter in preparing for his yearly call-to-battle, or lament for the fallen, or whatever it was he was trying to blast through the wheezy instrument he carried under his arm.

As I peeked out the window, I caught a glimpse of a struggling face, purple-hued and covered in a sheen of sweat. He looked like a Shriner at a community picnic trying to blow up balloons after a night of riding his little motorcycle up and down hotel corridors.

The fact that he was probably freezing to death couldn't have made his task any easier. Seven o'clock in the morning on November 11 in Sinterville, especially if you weren't wearing any knickers under your kilt, would have been a daunting experience for the hardiest of men—which this one definitely was not.

As my father bustled around in the kitchen, getting out cups and a bottle of whiskey, he kept badgering my mother to get the coffee going. Dad had never mastered the art of cooking.

The piper traipsed across the kitchen, trailing mud and wet grass behind him. Then he sheepishly retraced his steps, removed his brogans and swabbed up the mess with the mop my mother handed him. She'd make their coffee, but she wouldn't clean up after them.

His pipes groaning with relief as they were laid to rest in a corner, the piper thanked my father for the proffered "heart starter" in an accent so thick you could stir butterscotch with it. He then declined my mother's offer of breakfast in a soft croon that would have charmed the dew off the heather.

The neighbours had just had time to go back to sleep when the air was rent again, this time by a cacophony of car horns as the Sinterville and Wawa Brigade of the local Legion branch rolled up to our front door in whatever vehicles they had been able to commandeer for the occasion. There were, amongst others, a steam-belching old school bus, a contractor's dilapidated pickup, a battle-weary Jeep, and the Mudge Mongrel—a car Louie Mudge, a local mechanic, had built from cannibalized wrecks abandoned in fields throughout the area.

What I was witnessing was the first of a series of rituals

that would take place at our house every November 11, June 6, and on the anniversary of every other battle the "Old Sweats," as they called themselves, had ever fought in or even read about. My father didn't have a barn, but he had a piano, a repertoire of war songs and romantic ballads, and a couple of kids he'd taught to march into the living room at a given signal, wooden rifles on our shoulders, singing such crowd-pleasers as "Old Soldiers Never Die" and "Now Is The Hour."

From our point of view, these events were quite lucrative once you got over your initial stage fright. After we finished our songs, there wouldn't be a dry eye in the house and we'd find our pockets being stuffed with silver, and even folding money. Our parents would siphon off a fair amount of our take in the days ahead when they ran out of cash for cigarettes and a few staples like milk and bread, but there was usually enough left over to pay for a Saturday afternoon movie or two and a bag of licorice jawbreakers and soft caramels.

In fact, the assaults on Fort Douglas would have been fun if the revellers had known when to quit. But the 11 a.m. veterans' parade and ceremony, plus the obligatory afternoon at the Legion hall swapping jugs of draft beer and kitbags of war memories, were only necessary interruptions in the all-day party at our house.

Late in the afternoon, the piper would be back on our lawn, this time joined by the trumpeter who'd played "Taps" at the ceremony, and they'd involve themselves in a contest to see who could blow the loudest and the most off key. To hear their rendition of "Amazing Grace" was, well, truly amazing.

Incensed neighbours would call the local police detachment and, before long, the officer dispatched to issue a

warning to the revellers would be joining in the singsong—
beer in hand—along with the neighbours. I don't know how
the booze held out for so long. My parents certainly couldn't
have afforded to supply it. My guess is that whenever rations
got low, someone would pass the hat for funds, and they'd
select the drunkest among them to drive the ten miles there
and back to the Legion to replenish the stock.

Each of us kids had a secret perch where we could sit
unobserved and watch the carryings-on. We'd compare
notes in the morning and could have made a fortune out
of selling the material to the tabloids or blackmailing the
participants if we'd owned a Polaroid camera.

But the parties took their toll on us youngsters. We'd go
to bed wired from the second-hand smoke we'd inhaled,
the sips of beer that had been foisted on us by well-mean-
ing celebrants, and the buzz brought on by the constant
pounding of the piano, adults shouting to be heard, and the
dim awareness that you weren't witnessing something that
normal people usually took part in.

If you were lucky, you fell asleep right away. Otherwise,
you'd hear the party slide into a bear pit of imagined slights,
hurt feelings, hurled threats, invitations to step outside, the
occasional brawl on the lawn, and then a deathly silence as
the crowd dispersed into the night.

The following morning offered the fractured stillness of
a worked-over battlefield. The upended lamps would have
been righted, the debris from spilled glasses, overflowing
ashtrays, and broken records cleared away, and life would
gradually return to normal.

But after some time had elapsed and frayed nerves had
had a chance to mend, someone would one day discover that
the Battle of Knackwurst Ridge had occurred on that date
and the whole thing would start all over again.

Until I was old enough to know better, I thought there was a typographical error in the Legion motto and that it really should have read "Lets We Forget."

Why else, I reasoned, would normally sane and sensible people—at least by the standards I'd been exposed to—go to such lengths to try to eradicate every last memory of the war years?

Chapter Six
THE MAGIC OF CHRISTMAS

Everyone who grew up believing in Santa Claus, the star in the East, and the babe born in a manger has a favourite Christmas memory.

Perhaps it's the year that the weather and the transportation networks cooperated, allowing the entire family to get together in time to open their gifts and sit down at the dinner table for turkey and all the trimmings.

Or maybe it's the time Uncle Bill, fortified by a generous intake of eggnog, climbed onto the roof and hollered "Ho, ho, ho!" down the chimney—sending a pack of wide-eyed kids scurrying for their beds.

Still others might remember with great fondness the Christmas Eve the snowflakes were at their fattest and laziest, the fire crackled on cue in the fireplace, and the right person was snuggled up on the sofa sharing a hot apple cider and a kiss or two.

My favorite Christmas memory—one I'll cherish for as long as there is breath enough in me to whistle "Silver Bells"—is an image of my mother standing on a snow-covered garbage dump in Wawa.

My mother was the female counterpart of Peter Pan—a little girl who never grew up. Christmas to her, even her last one, when she spent most of her time hiding just how sick she really was, meant poring over department store catalogues for weeks to make sure the perfect gift for everyone was on her ever-expanding list, practising restraint by not putting the tree up before December 10, and fussing over grocery lists to make certain she had all the ingredients for everyone's favourite dish.

She once confessed that she was twelve years old before she stopped believing in Santa Claus. I think she was telling a little white lie. I don't think she ever stopped believing.

And so, to that snow-covered garbage dump. It was December 24, and I was eight that year while my brothers were five and three. None of us remembers the incident personally, but it was confirmed to us time and again over the years by townsfolk who came to regard it as their own *Gift of the Magi* story.

My mother, as usual, had finished her catalogue Christmas shopping weeks early. The various gifts that had been shipped north by rail from Sault Ste. Marie she had salted away in cardboard boxes in our back shed. Unfortunately, that ramshackle structure was also the storage area for the cartons and paper bags of trash that were collected whenever the town council could free up a dump truck to make the rounds.

As fate would have it, collection time that week was just before dusk on Christmas Eve. My father, who had obviously made more than a few trips to the punchbowl at that afternoon's office party, was counting tipsy sheep on the living room sofa when the garbage truck arrived.

The driver, who considered himself a construction worker

and not a garbage collector, leaned heavily on the horn. This was the signal that if you wanted your garbage hauled away, you had better throw it on the back of the truck before he lost his patience and drove away.

My mother managed to rouse my father long enough for him to stagger to the back shed and grab hold of every box and bag in sight. His chore completed, he repaired to the sofa once again and continued his pastoral inventory.

As the story goes, my mother managed to bathe and bed down three excited youngsters after several readings of *The Night Before Christmas*, then headed for the back shed to retrieve the long-hidden Christmas gifts and spread them under the tree.

What greeted her was beyond the Grinch's wildest dreams. There wasn't so much as a little toy drum left in the shed. By now, all the stores were closed for the holidays and even if they'd been open, all the dollars lovingly hoarded over the past eleven months had gone to buy money orders made out to far-off catalogue stores.

Few people in post-war Wawa had a telephone, let alone a car, so the teenaged daughter of our next-door neighbour was pressed into service as babysitter, and my mother set out on foot for a diner half a mile down the road, where she knew she could use the telephone.

Once there, she called the local Ontario Provincial Police detachment and related the story to Constable Orrie Waito. He was there within minutes and drove my mother to the dump.

From her vantage point on one snow-covered pile of trash, she was able to spot that day's haul, since it hadn't snowed in the previous twenty-four hours, and the bags and boxes were heaped up where the dump truck had deposited them.

With the cruiser's headlights and Constable Waito's flash-light illuminating the area, my mother began a bare-handed search through every container in sight. The truck driver had obviously cut a few corners in his haste to get home for Christmas Eve because there wasn't that much trash to paw through. It soon became evident that our gifts were nowhere to be found.

My mother returned home in tears. Even her hitherto-unshakeable belief in the magic of Christmas had been dented by the events of the previous few hours. My father, waking up long enough to hear my mother's tale of woe, went back to sleep assuring her that Santa would take care of everything.

And Santa did just that. Within the hour, there was a knock on the door and Constable Waito, an ear-to-ear smile on his beefy face, stood there with a large box containing all the gifts my mother had ordered from the catalogues.

Employing deductive reasoning that would have done Sherlock Holmes proud, the policeman had gone back to the diner and quizzed the short-order cook as to who was within earshot when my mother had telephoned him. The cook remembered that one fellow had lit out of there like a singed reindeer, and it turned out he had made a beeline for the town dump in his pickup truck.

The only thing that shocked my ever-trusting mother more than the fact that someone would overhear her conver-sation and head out to scoop up our Christmas presents was that Constable Waito might expect her to lay charges against the culprit. And at Christmastime, for heaven's sake!

And there was icing on the Christmas cake that year too. When one of Wawa's leading merchants, Bernie Turcotte, heard about the plight of three youngsters who might not have any gifts under their Christmas tree, he went down to the dry goods store he had recently locked up for the holidays and grabbed toys, games, and clothing off his shelves. He showed up on our doorstep just after Constable Waito (now off duty) had left with a couple of cups of whiskey-laced coffee under his belt.

"What the hell, I had so much fun collecting this stuff, I'm not going to take it back," Bernie said when he heard the news from my mother that our gifts had been recovered. "Let them have a double Christmas this year."

Little did any of them know that it would be a double Christmas every year from then on with the retelling of the story of just how far people in a little snowbound northern village were willing to go to help Santa make his appointed rounds.

Chapter Seven
ROCKY TAKES A FALL

Y ou'll never know what being really miserable is until you've had to sit in an unheated outhouse in forty-below weather. And I'm talking Fahrenheit, where water freezes at thirty-two degrees above the zero mark.

When two Northerners meet in the depths of winter, they mumble through their lip hair, "Cold enuf fer ya?" If both of them are men, they might add an expletive or two.

I can remember as a kid, waking up in the bedroom of our clapboard house in Sinterville with my hair frozen to the wall because the space heater in the living room, our only source of heat, had run out of oil overnight. On those days, it was almost a pleasure to climb into frigid clothing and make the five-mile ride on a backfiring bus to our one-room schoolhouse in Wawa. At least it would be warm there. Until you had to answer nature's call.

A town that existed to serve the steel industry, Wawa had experienced something of a population boom during and immediately after the war years. This had created a problem of overcrowding at the one elementary school in the area.

Somebody got the bright idea of turning an old, tumble-down house nearby into a one-room annex, but through lack of funding or foresight, they didn't include indoor plumbing in their renovation plans. No problem. Over the weekend, they had someone throw up a two-hole outhouse. No insulation. No lighting. No running water. Just a box-like affair inside a shack.

And since little kids were considered dumber and thus more compliant than bigger kids, it was the first few grades that inherited the annex and outhouse, while the rest of the students continued to enjoy the relative comforts of indoor plumbing and temperatures that stayed around seventy degrees.

The school board, in its benevolence, passed a motion one particularly dark and stormy night that if ever the temperature dropped to minus fifty degrees, the schools would not open that day. Since Wawa is virtually on the same line of latitude as the Siberian Lowlands, this used to happen fairly frequently from mid-December until the April thaw.

But oh those days when that stubborn thermometer hovered at minus forty-five and you had to begin the ritual of dressing for the bone-chilling walk along that icy gauntlet from your front door to the bus stop. Undershirt. Underpants. Longjohns. Two pairs of thick socks. Flannel sportshirt. Heavy flannel breeches we called "breeks," held up by elastic suspenders. A thick woollen sweater. Hockey toque pulled down over the forehead. Plaid woollen parka with fleece-trimmed hood. Mismatched plaid scarf over mouth and nose and tied behind the head. Two pairs of home-knitted mittens. Black rubber boots.

When the unheated bus discharged its cargo of frost-bitten zombies, Miss Grexton, our teacher, began the tedious ritual of peeling off the outer layers of Arctic survival gear so that we could take out our readers and learn all about Mother baking an apple pie for Dick and Jane and Baby Sally, who lived on a sunny street somewhere in Middle America.

Is it any wonder that as the big hand of the chipped enamel alarm clock on Miss Grexton's desk inched its way past twelve again and again, no human hand shot up seeking permission to leave the room? It was safer to sit rooted to the spot than to go through the contortions of getting dressed again for the elements. If an "accident" didn't happen as you struggled with the zipper on your parka, the shockwave of hitting that first blast of cold air outside the classroom could cause you to lose control of whichever internal organ you'd been clenching with all your might.

Miss Grexton kept soap and a washcloth plus a supply of nondescript underwear and unisex pantaloons at the back of the room where a hapless victim of equipment failure could clean up behind a curtained-off area. I can still see poor little Agnes Williams blubbering at her desk while a puddle slowly formed on the linoleum floor beneath her. Her fate would be to clean herself up as best she could behind the curtain, don the hideous garb the seniors called the "Oh-Oh Uniform" and sit in embarrassed numbness for the balance of the day while her clothes dried with a malodorous hiss on the space heater in the corner.

That sharp, distinct smell of soggy clothing drying as you sat in lepers' rags and, even worse, the taunts of your fellow pupils on the long, mortifying bus ride home were great deterrents against any of us allowing accidents of that sort to happen.

However, on the days when you'd slept late and had to wolf down your Cream of Wheat, giving your home bathroom a miss in order to make the bus, you'd arrive at school feeling like a condemned man on the day of his execution, knowing that it was only a matter of time before you had to take that long and fateful walk.

There are people who will tell you that the cry of a timber wolf is enough to strike fear in the heart of even the bravest of men. There are others who panic at the sight of a shark's fin knifing through the water. But to a little boy in the days of primitive latrines, the thing that sent a shiver of cold terror racing through his veins was the jolt of awareness that the moment to pay a visit to the outhouse had arrived.

On those occasions, Miss Grexton, bless her heart, didn't stand on ceremony. Your mad dash for the door was excused and understood even though you hadn't raised your hand to ask for permission to leave. With shouts of "We know where you're going" ringing in your ears, you headed straight for the little shack in the clearing, covering the distance in a hop, skip, and jump that would have won a blue ribbon at the fall fair.

Once inside, you stripped down faster than a battle-weary soldier on an eight-hour Parisian furlough and hopped up onto the bum-numbing plank with the two circular holes cut in it. The only nice thing about having to go in winter was that the wood was frozen solid so you didn't come away with splinters, like you did in September or June.

And you didn't dawdle. There's no greater incentive to getting things over with in a hurry than the knowledge that you're slowly freezing to death and you probably have about five minutes total before someone will have to come along and chip you off your perch.

But an even worse pitfall, in the truest sense of the word, of having to race to the "Jack Out Back" (as the seniors called it because it wasn't fancy enough to be referred to as a "John") was discovered one blustery afternoon by my friend and classmate Rocky Mitchell.

I was seated at my desk, staring out the window at the whirling snow and mentally mushing my team of huskies to the nearest outpost with a bottle of life-saving medicine in a leather pouch slung over my shoulder. Suddenly, I became aware of every head in the room turning my way and Miss Grexton standing there with a slight smile on her face, waiting for my reply.

"I was asking you, my little daydreamer, if you'd mind going to see what's keeping Rocky," she repeated. "He's been gone an awfully long time."

One of the drawbacks of being the teacher's pet, other than suffering vicious teasing from jealous classmates, was that she often recruited you to take on a less-than-pleasant task. This time, for instance, it meant struggling into breeches, boots, jacket, and toque and trudging through sub-zero weather to see why the kid who sat behind me hadn't returned from his solitary sojourn.

After a hazardous five-hour trek, that in reality lasted about thirty seconds, I reached the outpost, having had to shoot and eat all my sled dogs along the way. Well, okay, I actually polished off the remains of a peanut butter sandwich I'd found in my jacket pocket. I scrabbled the wooden door of the outhouse open with ice-numbed fingers and peered inside the unlit cubical. Where Rocky should have been sitting in frigid misery, there were two empty "thrones." Too young to realize there was anything amiss, I let the spring-loaded door slam back into place and turned to run back to the welcoming warmth of the classroom with the news that Rocky wasn't where he was supposed to be.

Luckily for him, the perpetually howling wind died down just then, and I heard a faint, eerie call for help from inside the ice palace. Prying open the door once again, I tentatively called out, "Rocky?" and almost ran for cover when I was answered by a disembodied voice wailing, "Down here!"

"Down here" went beyond my worst nightmares. It was coming from the depths of the two-holer. Either Rocky was down there or I was about to be grabbed by an evil spirit that lived in outhouses and turned bad little boys into...

My curiosity out-wrestled my grisly imagination, and I sidled up to the raised wooden box upon which a drunken carpenter had nailed two toilet seats. Peering down one of them, I could barely make out a moving object in the murky depths.

"Rocky, is that you?" I whispered. It didn't dawn on me until later that any goblin worth the name would have answered in the affirmative just to lure me closer.

"Yes, it's me. Get me out of here," was the less than cheerful reply.

The rest of the scene is a bit of a blur. I remember running back into the classroom and announcing in a loud voice that caused Miss Grexton to suck in all of the room's available oxygen and clutch at her bosom, "Rocky's at the bottom of the shithouse!"

I clapped a hand over my mouth but it was too late. I'd blurted out our schoolyard appellation for the outdoor privy in the heat of the moment. The urgency of my message got her attention. I recall Miss Grexton running out in the snow in the teacher's laced-up high-heeled oxfords to confirm my findings, then across a drift-encrusted field to the nearest house hightailing it at a pace that would have done my favourite football player Elroy "Crazy Legs" Hirsch proud.

Somebody found a ladder and, having raised the entire wooden topping of the two-holer, climbed down to pluck a near-frozen Rocky out of the bottom of the pit. I braced myself for the outpouring of admiration that would surely come my way for what I'd done. I just hoped the senior boys would be careful when they hoisted me onto their shoulders. But for some strange reason, Rocky got all the attention.

A few days later, once his hero status had faded and Rocky had deigned to give us all the gory details of his journey to the centre of the earth, I learned that a new Christmas sweater had caused the whole thing.

Holding off until the last possible moment, Rocky had finally answered the urgent call of nature by dashing out of the classroom clad only in the clothes he'd been wearing. He'd whipped off his sweater on the way to the latrine so that he could pull down the braces holding up his heavy woollen trousers just before he hopped up onto the right-hand seat.

With more urgent matters on his mind, he'd absent-mindedly tossed the sweater to his left, only to realize in horror that it had dropped into the other hole. Terrified that his parents would punish him for losing his brand-new sweater, Rocky had squeezed down the hole, trying to emulate Errol Flynn in the movie *Robin Hood* by swooping down to snag the sweater in his outstretched hand while hanging on to the rim of the toilet seat with the other. But he wasn't Errol Flynn, and he dropped knee-deep into half-frozen sludge. He was still clutching the befouled pullover in his blue fingers when they hauled him out.

As still happens after an institutional near-tragedy, the powers-that-be overreacted to prevent a recurrence of Rocky's fall from grace. From that day forward, trips to the outhouse were made in tandem. If Freddy Scafe had to go, Donny Bernardo was enlisted to ride shotgun on the trip. If Ginny Haynes needed to be excused, Carol Carter acted as her lady-in-waiting. Rocky Mitchell and I spent the rest of the school year learning more than either of us wanted to know about each other's personal habits.

To this day, I can't help wondering whether the other graduates of Miss Grexton's class of 1948 still check off a warm, solitary, lockable bathroom when they run down a mental list of their greatest blessings.

Chapter Eight

DOC MACTAVISH AND THE SIX-YEAR MOLAR

My dad and I had our first beer together when I was seven years old. A dozen years or so would pass before we got around to having the next one.

In addition to being too young to remember much, I was in a state of shock at the time, brought on by paroxysms of physical pain in my jaw. So my recollection of the incident has probably evolved more from family tellings of the story than actual recall on my part.

I do remember Dad trying to make me laugh by taking the glass of beer he'd just poured and blowing the foam into my face. Even at my tender age, I realized this was a clumsy but well-intentioned effort to distract me from my predicament. I remember thinking it was nice to be sitting there laughing with my dad and I tried a grin, but the movement caused another stab of pain in my lower mandible.

Our boys' night out took place at the staff house of the Helen Mine on the outskirts of Wawa. The only perk of my father's job as timekeeper at the mine was a key to the small house that middle management used as a lunchroom, rec centre, and dormitory on nights when their work kept them late or the weather was too brutal to try to make it home.

There was a small refrigerator in the kitchen where you could buy bottled beverages on the honour system. After my ordeal, Dad took me over there and introduced me to his panacea for all of life's physical and emotional ills—a bottle of beer.

I don't think I drank much of it, but I remember the pain went away.

Anyway, the reason my dad found it necessary to try to dull the searing pain in my jaw was that I had just become the latest victim of Wawa's shoddy medical system. No one in his right mind, least of all a professional man, would voluntarily set up practice in this hardrock mining town, with its well-earned reputation, in the years following World War II, as a raucous, blackfly-plagued, facility-deprived quagmire.

Idle gossip, the town's second-largest yield of raw material, had it that Doc MacTavish had arrived one day by train in the late 1930s and holed up in the beverage room of the Lakeview Hotel for several weeks until he was satisfied nobody had followed him. No one ever learned what sort of medical misdeeds he might have perpetrated up to that point. Only those he was about to.

In a haphazard way that couldn't happen in today's highly regulated society, Doc MacTavish eventually became Wawa's only medical practitioner. And veterinarian. And dentist. Whether anyone ever asked him to produce credentials is academic because he's been dead for close to fifty years. As have most of his patients, man and beast alike.

The majority of the inhabitants of Wawa went to Doc MacTavish as a last resort. The owners of the mine provided him with a small clinic next door to the staff house, but he preferred to spend most of his waking hours at the Lakeview.

It was with great reluctance that anyone called him out of the beer parlour to perform minor surgery that couldn't be done at his regular table. Have you ever had a dislocated shoulder put back in its socket or a gash on your leg sewn up by a cranky, shaky doctor, anxious to get back to his regular haunt before the head on his glass of beer has dissipated?

And he was a better doctor than he was a dentist. My dad was once pressed into service as Doc MacTavish's assistant when the old fellow had sprained his wrist (your guess is as good as mine) and couldn't pull teeth. I remember Dad, whose wrists were the strongest in town because he pounded a manual typewriter all day long, marvelling over supper one night about how he'd followed Doc MacTavish's instructions and had yanked out a miner's tooth.

"Only he'd directed me to pull the wrong one," my father remarked, still shaken by the incident. "I thought the miner would pick me up and throw me through the nearest wall, but he just laughed and told me to make sure I got the right one on the next try."

So when I was stricken with a severe toothache one night, my folks tried all the home remedies: oil of cloves, cigarette smoke blown directly onto the tooth, and a hot water bottle applied to the cheek. When nothing worked, it was decided that Doc MacTavish would have to be pressed into action.

My dad found the old gentleman picking pink and green spiders out of his beer glass, and persuaded him to take me up to the clinic to have the offending tooth removed. They say that, until the day the dentist chair was thrown on the scrap heap, you could still see the ridges where my fingers had gripped the arms in sheer agony.

"Oh, my God, Mel, I didn't realize it," the good doctor exclaimed to my father as the offending tooth finally parted from my jaw. "I thought it was a baby tooth. It's a six-year-molar that came in bad. I would've given the little guy freezing if I'd known that!"

Thus my trip to the staff house and my first sip of beer as my dad tried to find a way to stifle my sobs of pain and his feelings of guilt for allowing Doctor Dipso to get his hands on me.

Next morning, I decided to get whatever mileage I could out of my war wound. Bursting into my classroom, I hooked my index finger into the corner of my mouth and proudly displayed the gap in my bottom row of teeth to Miss Grexton, the teacher I adored.

"So that's what all the commotion was about last night," she said, peering over rimless glasses. "They say you could hear the screaming all the way down to the lake."

You wouldn't think it would take much time to take your finger out of your mouth, make an about turn and walk sheepishly to your desk amidst the catcalls of fellow pupils. I figured at the time that it took at least an hour.

I'd imagined Miss Grexton would have at least clucked her tongue, murmured, "There, there," and allowed as how I must have been a brave little man to go through such pain. One daydream on the bus to school that morning had even conjured up a scene of her laying my fevered brow on her bosom.

And I'd been sure that the wound was sufficient for Ginny Haynes and Carol Carter to smile prettily through their tears at me while I manfully took my seat.

I'd envisioned Bruce McDermid slapping me on the back at recess and saying with a stiff upper lip, "Well done old man. The boys and I have been thinking about asking you to join us in our treehouse. We can use another brave member in our gang."

When none of these fantasies came to pass, I had to console myself with the fact that at least the treacherous molar had been worth two bucks to an overly generous tooth fairy.

Chapter Nine

THE NIGHT THEY ALMOST BLEW US ALL TO KINGDOM COME

M y dad wasn't one for doing chores around the house. Popping the cap off a beer with the Nazi belt buckle somebody had made into a bottle opener and dumping the occasional overflowing ashtray into the toilet, to his way of thinking, put him in line for the *Helpful Hubby of the Year* award. But when you lived in Sinterville, in the northern wilderness, in the late 1940s, there was one duty you had to perform or you and your family froze to death.

The clapboard shacks some contractor with a sick sense of humour and the soul of a successful criminal lawyer had thrown up and called houses were each equipped with a living room space heater. These glorified steel drums guzzled fuel oil like a Russian-built tractor and had to be filled nightly to battle winter's sub-zero temperatures.

All twenty-three of Sinterville's weatherbeaten dwellings had a shack out back containing a fifty-gallon drum with a spigot from which you transferred oil into a five-gallon can. You then fetched the can into the house to fill the stove's ever-thirsty holding tank.

My dad hated the job, and his litany of curses as he donned parka and galoshes to stagger out to the shed became a routine part of our pre-dinner table talk. On the nights when he was on a seventy-two-hour bender and didn't come home, the task fell to my mother and to me and my brother Greg, as soon as we were big enough to heft the metal container onto a toboggan, pull it to the porch, and bump it up one step at a time to the back door. To this day, I feel sick whenever I get a whiff of fuel oil.

Anyway, the fifty-gallon drum needed frequent replenishing, and this was done by a Frick and Frack team of oil deliverymen. They always managed to drive over a wayward toboggan or painstakingly crafted snowman in our backyard as part of the routine of filling the drum with a hose they wheeled off their tank truck.

One particularly gloomy night, Frick and Frack were late making their rounds and came screeching into our yard, knocking down my mother's fully-laden clothesline pole in their haste to make their last delivery and head for hearth and home—or, more likely, the beer parlour at Joe Perkovich's Lakeview Hotel.

Their job completed, they waved cheerily at my father as he walked to the shed, grinding the family's freshly laundered clothing under their truck wheels as they sped away.

Shivering and cursing as the wind blew a gust of airborne snow down the neck of his jacket, my dad quickly filled the five-gallon can and carried it into the living room in preparation for filling the stove.

Exhausted from this Herculean labour, he struggled out of his jacket and cap and decided that before hoisting the can up to the gaping maw of the stove's holding tank, he would hoist a beer to his perennially parched lips.

That little decision saved our lives.

By the time the beer had disappeared—he was slow that night and it took more than thirty seconds—my mother had dinner on the table and insisted we all sit down to eat while the food was still hot.

Dad protested that he was just about to fill the stove, but it was empty bluster. He wanted to fill the stove about as much as he wanted to mush a team of huskies cross-country to Mukluk Harbour for a temperance rally. And besides, my mother could be fairly firm when it came to getting the family to sit down together for a meal.

As usual, we buzz-sawed through the pot roast and side vegetables. Nothing whips up an appetite better than a howling wind shaking the house and threatening to hurl you out into the elements on an empty stomach. Greg and I were arguing with each other about whose turn it was to get the one maraschino cherry that had been placed in each can of fruit cocktail by a miserly Libby's employee when a frantic knock sounded on our back door.

This brought the hubbub to an instant halt. Nobody in Sinterville made social calls on a winter's evening when the perpetual blizzard made walking more than ten feet in any one direction a major trek.

My mother and father glanced at each other as if this was a dreaded visit from the Gestapo. Rising stealthily from his chair, my dad inched towards the door, which by now was threatening to fly off its hinges from the beating it was taking.

Shrugging resignedly, he flung the door open and was greeted by the huge bulk of Frick the oilman, whose face was whiter than the snowflakes that clung to his fur cap.

"Oh my god, Mel," he blurted. "Am I ever glad to see you're still alive!"

Helping the distraught man to the chair he'd just vacated,

my dad followed up by handing him his sure-fire cure for all of life's emergencies, a bottle of beer. After a couple of quick swallows, Frick explained that before making their last delivery to our house, he and his partner had offloaded fifty gallons of gasoline to a machine shop down the road.

In their hurry to get the day's work done, they'd forgotten to switch back to their truck's fuel oil tank and they'd filled our drum with straight gasoline.

"If we hadn't realized our mistake and turned around in time, you people would have all been blasted to kingdom come," Frick said with a weak chuckle that he quickly suppressed when he saw that no one else was getting the joke.

Now some men would have gotten angry and knocked the oilman off the chair for putting his family at such risk. But that wasn't my dad's style.

Having listened to Frick's plea not to complain to his boss or he and his partner would lose their jobs, Dad struck a bargain. There was no question that a new barrel of fuel oil would be delivered that night, no matter how long the oilmen took to get it there.

And since Frick and Frack had put us in harm's way, it was only fair, Dad allowed, that they prove when they delivered the new barrel that it contained fuel oil by filling our stove themselves.

In fact, he allowed as how he'd consider it right neighbourly if they dropped by each night as they finished their rounds and filled the stove as a way of making amends for giving us such a fright.

With casually dropped threats, and a round or two of beer, my dad managed to string out this act of contrition until the first flock of wild geese had flown north over our house and the space heater had been shut down for a well-deserved four-month layoff.

Chapter Ten

WASHED UP AT NINE

Not many people can brag that they had a well-paid job at seven years of age. Nor that they engaged in bitter labour negotiations at the age of eight and won—only to be washed up and penniless a short time later.

Well, it happened to me.

It was the dead of winter when our family arrived in Sinterville in the mid-1940s. By the time our brains had thawed, the next fall had rolled around, and I found myself attending school in Wawa, five miles and a bit down the road.

You see, Sinterville didn't have a school. It didn't, for that matter, have a store. And the only person who owned a car had been tinkering with it, trying to get it to run, since the outbreak of World War II had made spare parts as hard to come by as silk stockings.

The kids from Sinterville used to get to school aboard a decrepit old bus that wheezed its way between the village and Wawa whenever somebody remembered to make the run. You could hear it coming for miles, so you had plenty of time to get out to the road. There were no assigned bus stops. You simply stood there and the driver figured out that you were waiting for a ride into town. Most of the time anyway.

It was that bus that provided me with the transportation link for my meteoric rise in the world of commerce. I'd like to claim credit for the idea that brought me untold riches, but in all honesty the scheme was too complicated for someone my age to have concocted. When it all happened, I wasn't that many months away from finally having mastered the art of tying my own shoelaces without them coming loose and tripping me a few minutes later.

Actually, I owe the entire experience to Katie McCabe's hormones. Katie was in charge of the operation before me, but she had recently turned thirteen and had decided that making out after school with Jimmy Bishop up by the water tower north of the village was more fun than working.

It was the scandal of the week in Sinterville when Ken Richardson, the grocer, fired Katie because she'd failed to perform her duties three times in a row. My mother, or "Maw" as I sometimes called her after watching a western movie, poured tea and sympathy while Mrs. McCabe poured out her troubles at our kitchen table the day after the firing. Having done the neighbourly thing, my mother allowed her practical side to prevail as soon as a slightly mollified Mrs. McCabe had eaten the last butter tart and gone home.

Dressing me up in my finest overalls and giving my stubborn cowlick a quick comb, Maw hauled me out to the roadside and flagged down the next bus to Wawa. One of her carefully hoarded dimes went into the fare box to pay for her ride. Kids travelled free.

My mother never ceased to amaze me. Normally a fairly shy and standoffish person, she would come to life like an irrepressible press agent when an opportunity came our way.

On this particular occasion, she saw a chance to augment my father's meager take-home pay cheque, and there was no stopping her.

I don't remember many of the details after the bus had dropped us off in front of Richardson's Grocery Store and my mother had bearded the hapless proprietor in his den. Well, to be more precise, she'd found him up a ladder, stocking one of his shelves. The poor man didn't have a prayer. By the time he had reluctantly agreed to give an untried youngster like me a chance, Wawa's leading (and only) grocer was half-convinced that little Tommy Douglas was the next Timothy Eaton, Alexander Graham Bell, and Horatio Alger all wrapped up in one.

To be honest, a trained chimpanzee could have done the job. It consisted of walking around to the twenty-three houses in Sinterville twice a week after school. Since spelling wasn't my strong suit, I would simply hand each housewife (as they were called in those days) a pink pad of paper and a pencil. One after the other, they would write their name at the top of a page and fill in their grocery order. When I had visited all twenty-three houses, I would flag down the next bus and ride it into Wawa. The accommodating drivers would usually wait while I dropped the stack of grocery orders off at the store, and I'd be back in Sinterville in time for supper.

The next day, Ken Richardson would fill up the back of his pickup truck with the boxed orders and deliver them to the various Sinterville households that had requisitioned supplies.

It was the best job I've ever had. With no telephones or personal transportation available to them, the Sinterville housewives considered me a vital part of their domestic routine—and rewarded me accordingly. Each of them seemed to try to outdo the next in seeing who could best fill my chubby little cheeks with exotic pastries and sugary confections. I became quite adept at sniffing the wind and anticipating Mrs. Docharty's shortbread cookies or Mrs. Lepak's apple strudel.

And I even got paid for it! On his second run of the week, Ken would drop off my mother's order and reduce her bill by one dollar. I never saw the money, but at the end of a year, my folks ordered a brand-new bicycle from the Eaton's catalogue, and I was the envy of every kid in Sinterville when it arrived at the train station. It was the only bike I ever owned, and I rode it until it finally fell apart when I was fifteen years old.

Like all success stories, though, this one has a down side. Everything had been going well for just over a year. Ken Richardson was happy with the job I was doing, the housewives thought I was adorable, and I was quite content to continue shovelling in the calories while completing a chore that was easier than cleaning my room. Then Katie McCabe came back into the picture. She didn't want her old job back—she was still having too much fun with Jimmy—but she couldn't resist the chance to burst my bubble.

For reasons stated earlier, she was never home when I made my rounds. But one day I was later than usual and she was making her dishevelled way up her walk as I left with her mother's grocery order.

"I hear Ken Richardson's paying you a dollar to take his orders," she smirked. "He used to pay me two."

I tearfully told my mother this distressing news once I'd made the return trip from Wawa. She tried to brush off the whole thing by reminding me of my Sunday School lesson about the worker who was bitter that he'd agreed to work for a certain number of shekels only to find out that another worker had struck a better bargain. The parable hadn't made sense to me at the time and it still didn't. The knowledge that Katie McCabe had been paid twice as much as me festered inside me for a whole week.

"Is that why you've been looking so glum lately?" said Grocer Richardson when I finally blurted out my displeasure. "Well, you've been doing such a fine job I was thinking of giving you a raise anyway. Starting next week, I'll pay you two dollars too."

The victory made me giddy. I was too young to know much about labour negotiations, other than what I picked up from the disgruntled miners riding the bus at the end of their shifts, but here I'd just bargained a raise that had doubled my salary.

My euphoria, however, was short-lived. Before I could deliver the glad tidings to my family, my exuberant mother stopped me in my tracks with the news that my father had received a raise. We'd finally be able to afford the rent on a bigger house in Wawa. After the deprivation of Sinterville, it was like moving from Shantytown to Snob Hill.

But even though I'd be moving five miles or so down the road, I could still keep my job, couldn't I? I could hop the bus after school and head for Sinterville, do the rounds, and take the list back to the grocery store. This way I could just walk home from the store instead of facing another bus trip.

My mother hugged me to her bosom and told me what a little trouper I had been by helping out and all, but it wouldn't be necessary anymore. And besides, Wayne Walters, who lived next door to us, was a year older than me and his family really needed the money, so she'd talked it over with his mother who was all excited about Wayne taking over. And it really should be someone from the village who did the job after all.

Like John L. Lewis bargaining with the coal barons, I argued my case, visions of sugar cookies with wings dancing in my head. It wouldn't be fair—after so long a time sweating and straining twice a week, week in and week out, to build a rapport with the housewives and the grocer—to hand over the job to someone else. This emotional outburst was accompanied by a thumping of the side of my fist into my open palm.

If *they* didn't need the money anymore, I pointed out, they could give it to me. There were lots of things I could find to spend it on: sending away for an ant farm, buying a set of drums, saving up for a motorcycle that I would buy when I reached my teens. Looking back on it later, I realized that these arguments only made my parents more determined to hand the job off to someone else. I'm sure the mind picture of ants escaping the farm and wandering at will around the house, me banging away on a set of drums in a house with paper-thin walls, or a teenaged Tommy Douglas racing around Wawa on a souped-up motorcycle didn't do my cause a bit of good.

At any rate, Wayne Walters kept taking grocery orders for Ken Richardson until high school football practice started interfering. He eventually became a multi-millionaire in the mining industry and retired to the Bahamas while still a relatively young man.

I moved to Wawa with my family and took up an endless search for a job as comparatively easy, enjoyable, and rewarding as the one I'd left behind. That quest continues to this day.

I suppose there's a moral in this whole thing somewhere, but I'll be darned if I can figure out just exactly what it might be.

Chapter Eleven

TOMMY GOT HIS GUN

P ing.
 Ping.
Ping.

"Tommy, for crying out loud, stop it! Those things don't grow on trees you know. And you just destroyed an heirloom my great-grandmother brought over from Scotland. You either stop that right now or I'm taking that bloody gun away from you."

I knew my dad was bluffing. He'd destroyed that heirloom himself the year before. He'd accidentally knocked it off the Christmas tree after hoisting a little more than his usual quota of rye and water with some of his old army buddies who had shown up unannounced at our house on Christmas Eve. Dad could always perform his own version of the miracle of the loaves and fishes. Whenever a former comrade-in-arms or two came to visit, there was enough booze to go around, even if the cupboard had seemed bare just before their arrival.

"Aw, Mel, let him be," my mother retorted. "He's having

fun. You know he can't go out and play in that storm. He's been waiting for that gun for months. What's a few ornaments?"

The centrepiece of this family drama was the Daisy Red Ryder BB gun I had spotted in the Eaton's catalogue several weeks before. I had promptly announced with finality that it was the one present I wanted above all for Christmas.

My dad, to say the least, was displeased by this turn of events. Which was a real puzzlement to me because he had returned from the war not that long ago. He'd been a soldier, and soldiers had guns, didn't they? What's more, he had called me his little soldier in all those letters he had written from the front, wherever that was. This was really confusing because I loved my dad, despite some of the things he did when he was drinking. I wanted to be just like him. What was so bad about having a gun?

He actually tried to explain it to me. He said that, as an orderly room sergeant, he had never carried a gun himself. He told me that guns, any guns, were dangerous and he didn't want me to have one. Then he got all choked up and couldn't talk anymore.

When I asked my mother why Dad was so upset, she reminded me that he'd seen his best friend killed in the war and had promised himself that if he came back alive he would never have a gun in his house. She added that Dad wasn't really at his best these days because he was trying to cut down on his drinking, and he was having a bit of a hard time of it.

"But it's not a real gun," I argued. "I don't want to kill anything. I just want to shoot at targets and tin cans and that kind of stuff."

My mother smiled and said she'd see what she could do. But a strange thing happened. Over the days and weeks that followed, my dad remained adamant about not letting me have a BB gun. Nothing my mother could say would budge him. It was the first time that had ever happened. After a while, he relented a bit and said maybe I could have a popgun, but nothing that actually shot anything that could hurt anybody. To me, a popgun was something for little kids. I kept up my lobbying for the Daisy Company's top-of-the-line BB gun.

With only a few days to go before Christmas Eve, I was desperate. Dad still refused to entertain the idea of me getting a BB gun, and I was at risk of being teased by my friends, since I'd already told them I was getting one for Christmas. Both Gerry Johnson and Bruce McDermid had told me confidently that they were getting the Red Ryder special, and if I didn't have one I'd be out of the club. We didn't actually have a club, but Gerry had heard the expression "out of the club" somewhere, and it sounded so ominous I redoubled my efforts to get that gun.

Gerry was one year older than Bruce and me and, when I finally confessed that it looked like the BB gun was out of the question, he came up with the solution to my predicament. He had already shaken our faith in Santa Claus by telling us it was really our parents who put all the gifts under the tree. I didn't actually believe him, but when I woke up one time as my mother was putting a dime under my pillow and taking away a lost tooth, I started having my doubts. If there was no tooth fairy, could they have been lying to me and Greg all this time about Santa Claus?

Gerry suggested that his plan was foolproof. If all else failed, he said, tell your parents that you had asked Santa for the gun, and it would show up under the tree on Christmas Eve, especially if you hinted that you were doubting whether there was a Santa Claus after all. But then Gerry was also the guy who had told us that if we took a gold ring or brooch out of our mother's jewel box and set it on a piece of flypaper on St. Patrick's Day Eve, we'd catch a leprechaun, so I wasn't really counting on his latest piece of advice working either.

However, I figured I had nothing to lose, so when it looked like I had run out of options, I told my parents that I had written a letter to Santa and dropped it off at the post office on my way to school. A look passed between them at that point, and for the first time since I'd settled on the gun as my main Christmas gift, I thought I might have a shot at my dream coming true.

Years later, I was to learn that one of the reasons my mother hadn't put as much pressure on my dad as she might have to let me have the gun was that she had already spent all of her Christmas money buying presents from the catalogue. A BB gun would take a large bite out of the household budget. But somehow, when it became apparent that my Christmas would be less than merry if I didn't have that gun, she came up with the funds.

My joy knew no bounds that Christmas morning when I ran into the living room and there, tied up in a big red bow, was the Red Ryder BB gun I had been coveting for so long. I think I even kissed it.

The only disappointment was that a fierce snowstorm had struck overnight and the blizzard conditions precluded my going outside to set up one of the paper targets that came with the BB gun.

My mother, as must be fairly obvious by now, couldn't stand seeing a look of disappointment on her children's faces. She had had a Cinderella childhood herself—living with a less-than-loving grandmother from the age of eight, after her own mother had died. Her only dolls were cut-outs from magazines, and she and her sister—my aunt Betty—were expected to do all the housework, including scrubbing the pine floors throughout the house on hands and knees. They even had to pick out the splinters this job inevitably produced, all by themselves.

Thus, my mother's main purpose in life—other than loving my dad with a passion that died only when she did—was to make her kids' existence as pleasant as possible. So when I couldn't go outside to try out my new BB gun, my mother suggested I take a few pot shots at the ornaments hanging from the branches of our Christmas tree. Her reasoning was that replacing a few cheap baubles was a small price to pay for her son's happiness. Self-absorbed little twit that I was, I thought her idea was a terrific solution to the problem at hand.

But like all kids, I soon got bored with the game. It was so easy shattering the shiny balls that just hung there on the branch—especially once I found out I was a pretty fair shot—probably almost as good as Buffalo Bill Cody or Annie Oakley. And besides, my dad was ranting about how my mother was spoiling me rotten. I figured I should maybe put the gun away until the storm died down—both inside and outside our home.

It's really great when someone asks you to do something they think you won't want to do and you've already decided to do it anyway. That's what happened later Christmas Day when I was helping my mother prepare for Christmas dinner by cutting the raisins in half for the rice pudding that was a holiday tradition at our house. I suspected, rightly so as I found out years later, that Maw had invented the job of cutting raisins in half to keep me occupied while she was trying to get things ready. I had been bugging her to let me help and that's the job she'd come up with.

While she was making the pastry for another family

tradition, meat pies, she casually asked me if I would do her a big favour. Still infused with the Christmas spirit, I agreed without trying to get her to tell me what she wanted before promising to do her bidding.

"Well," she said softly, "I didn't realize how much it bothers your dad to see you firing that BB gun in the house. He has enough to handle at the moment, and I was wondering if you'd mind putting the gun away for a little while—at least until after we get Christmas out of the way."

The hug of gratitude I got when I came back to the kitchen after sliding the rifle under my bed was worth ten BB guns.

The winter storm that had set in Christmas morning took a full week to blow itself out. But New Year's Day dawned bright and sunny through the bedroom window. And there was something else I couldn't quite put my finger on at first that had my spirits soaring. Then it hit me. I didn't smell stale booze and the stench of overflowing ashtrays like I had on so many mornings since Dad got back from the war.

Where New Year's Eve over the past few years had been a mad blur of tipsy visitors turning into noisy drunks as the midnight hour approached, the previous night had seen my mother and father play 500 Rummy with another couple. A few beers had been consumed, but the loudest sound was friendly laughter, and the evening was over by 10:30 p.m.

It was a wonderful experience to get out of bed, put on my slippers and robe, and walk quietly through a living room that looked normal and not like the aftermath of a barroom brawl. Dad was sitting at the kitchen table reading a copy of *Ring Magazine*—he was a big boxing fan—and sipping a cup of coffee.

"Hi there, Tommy," he said with a bright smile. No hangover here. "I'm glad you're up. I've been thinking about your

BB gun, and I figured as long as you already have it you should learn how to use it safely. I've set up those bull's-eye targets that came with it and a few tin cans out on the back porch. After breakfast, I thought we could do a bit of target practice."

Despite his dislike of guns, Dad was a pretty fair shot. He explained that he had had to learn how to use a rifle during his training before he went to war. But he'd seen what guns could do and he couldn't help feeling that any weapon could only lead to violence. He made me promise that I would never point the BB gun at any living creature and that I would only use it for target practice.

I enjoyed that time with my father. I'd like to be able to say that a Christmas miracle had happened and that he stopped drinking completely. He didn't, of course, but he did cut down considerably. There was the odd fallback whenever his old army buddies dropped by. And he had a bit of a bad session when the anniversary of D-Day rolled around, but life gradually became a bit more normal in the Douglas household.

As for the BB gun, after I showed it to Gerry and Bruce to prove I really had gotten it for Christmas, I used it less and less frequently, finally leaving it under my bed for weeks at a time without thinking about it. Just like in the movies, where the hero finally hangs up his guns and decides to live a peaceful life, I had nothing more to prove.

Chapter Twelve
PLAYING WITH A DEAD FLY

As the bus lurched up the hill, I told myself it would soon be over. I hadn't cried yet, and I was determined to hang on.

The incantation began again, louder than before, "Tommy got the stra-ap. Tommy got the stra-ap!" The cruel, childish cadence divided the dreaded word into two stinging syllables.

My palms still tingled from the half-dozen staccato swipes of the wooden ruler each had taken. My cheeks still tingled with the flush of embarrassment the incident had caused.

My whole world had come crashing in on me just before school ended for the day. Two of the three loves of my young life had betrayed me within minutes of each other. The emotional pain far outstripped the throbbing in my hands.

The relic that masqueraded as a school bus finally sagged to a merciful halt in front of my house. The chant grew louder as I walked the gauntlet from the rear of the vehicle to the front entrance. Bruce McDermid stuck his foot out into the aisle, but I'd already learned that lesson the hard way and deftly stepped over the impromptu booby trap.

The driver, who had been watching me in the rearview mirror, yanked the handle that levered the double doors open and whispered, "Nice going, kid! You didn't shed a tear," as I stoically descended the short stairwell and stepped onto the gravel road.

The bus belched blue smoke as it trundled away. Several of its young riders tried to catch my attention by hanging halfway out the lowered side windows and yelling my name. I ignored them, staring straight ahead as I walked up our wooden front steps.

Once inside the sanctity of our front porch, I collapsed in a heap and began sobbing uncontrollably, hot tears welling up from miniature cauldrons that had been threatening to spill their contents for the past hour or so.

My mother was there instantly—I'd been counting on it—sweeping me up in her arms and clutching me to her bosom. At her gentle urging, I blurted out the horrible truth. "I-I-I got the-the strap," I stuttered moistly, the shame of it all sending me into further paroxysms of howls and snuffles.

A cool washcloth appeared like magic, and I found myself being lulled into a familiar state of well-being as my mother told me I was home now and everything was okay. Her hypnotically soothing voice calmed me to the point where I could relate, between hiccups, the terrible afternoon I'd put in.

It had all started out so well. One of the two most-sought-after rewards for good behaviour Miss Grexton meted out each day—the other being wiping the blackboards clean— was to stand on a chair at the front of our schoolhouse and watch out the window for the bus that would take us Sinterville residents home from our day at school in Wawa.

The bus would make its way down from the Helen Mine and along Wawa's main street past the school grounds.

As the vehicle appeared at the left-hand side of the school window, this was the designated lookout's cue to shout, "There goes the bus!"

That was the signal for the Sinterville pupils to begin racing to the cloakroom to don whatever outer clothing the season dictated. Sometimes it would be no more than a light windbreaker, baseball cap, and a pair of odiferous sneakers. And once the girls were ready, it was the boys' turn.

In the depths of winter, however, it meant hauling on heavy breeches, jacket, scarf, mittens, and boots. Miss Grexton looked small and frail standing in front of the class, but she could wrestle ten youngsters into winter gear faster than a jumpmaster hustling a group of first-time paratroopers up to the hitch line.

By the time everyone was bundled up, the bus would have made its loop around Wawa's downtown and would appear at the right side of the window. This prompted the litany, "Here she comes!" to be passed down from the observer to each would-be passenger in turn, like a water bucket along a fire line. Everyone would then pile out the school doors to board the vehicle for the ride to Sinterville.

If, for some inexplicable reason, the lookout missed the bus's appearance at the left side of the window as it belched its way towards Wawa's inner core, there was absolutely no way Miss Grexton could get everyone ready once the bus emerged on the right side of the window on its way to Sinterville. It was years before it dawned on me that if the old rattletrap had kept to some sort of schedule, there would have been no need for a lookout and no embarrassing scenario like the one I was about to experience.

For years after the incident, I would still wake up in a cold sweat when I dreamt about the day I caused the whole Sinterville contingent to miss the bus. This indiscretion meant we all had to wait for more than half an hour, while the vehicle made its trek to Sinterville and back again.

I've been hammered in the guts, literally and figuratively, a number of times since then, but I don't think any of those incidents caused greater consternation than the horror of seeing the bus I was supposed to spot coming down the road from the left actually edging into my peripheral vision from the right.

When I blurted out the horrible truth, Miss Grexton folded her arms over her chest, a sure sign of her annoyance, and asked how this state of affairs could possibly have happened.

Before I could plead my innocence, Carol Carter, who had just that morning sworn her undying love for me at recess, volunteered the information that she had seen me playing with a dead fly on the window sill when I was supposed to be watching for the bus.

Miss Grexton, whom I worshipped, made it a double heartbreak by unceremoniously removing me from the chair I'd been standing on while looking out the window and replacing me as lookout with my arch-rival Bruce McDermid. He, of course, didn't fail at his appointed task of spotting the bus the next time it appeared from the left.

Having slunk back to my seat to await the return of the wayward Sinterville Streak, I vaguely heard Miss Grexton warning the now-unruly class that the next person to talk out of turn would receive a dozen whacks of her ever-present wooden ruler. No sooner had this threat been issued than the traitorous Carol whispered to me that I really should have been paying attention to my duties instead of playing with a dead fly.

Chivalrous to a fault, I tried to warn Carol in what I believed was a similar whisper that Miss Grexton had just said she'd strap the next person who broke the silence.

"Tommy, was that you I heard talking?" Miss Grexton snapped. "Come up to my desk this instant."

In mentally replaying the angst of the following few minutes, I always see a look of pained resignation on Miss Grexton's face as she delivers the coup de grâce to the tentatively outstretched hands of her pet pupil. In later life, I too have made sweeping threats to youngsters within my charge, only to be backed into a corner of no return when my favourite stepped across the verbal line I had drawn in the sand.

However, even if she regretted what she had to do, Miss Grexton broke a little boy's heart when she carried out a threat she had probably uttered in a moment of exasperation.

But a little boy's heart mends quickly. The next day, when Carol Carter told me how brave I had been and how I had only been trying to protect her, I was as good as new.

The small collection of houses below the sulphur-belching sinter plant constitutes the community of Sinterville

Sinterville was just a small collection of houses near the sinter plant. The author's house was in the middle of the top row

Toddler Tom Douglas with his parents in Sault Ste. Marie before his Dad went to war

The author took his job as "man of the house" seriously by shovelling snow while his Dad was overseas

The author and his mother Dorene enjoy a happy moment in Sault Ste. Marie while his Dad is overseas

The author and brother Greg (with his white boots) after learning they will be leaving Sault Ste. Marie for Sinterville

The author (holding toboggan) and brother Greg in front of their Sinterville home with sinter plant in background

The author (right) and brother Greg in front of their Sinterville house with the sinter plant in the background

Brothers Greg (left) Tom (middle) and Norm
Douglas with dog Tuffy on the back steps of their
Sinterville home

The author (right) and brother Greg with "the murderer" (aka their father Mel) on the beach in Wawa

(Left to right) Brothers Norm, Greg and Tom Douglas enjoy a rare sunny day during a Sinterville winter

Springtime in Sinterville with (left to right) brothers Greg, Tom and Norm Douglas playing on a melting snowbank

The author's mother, Dorene, on a Sinterville
snowbank with dog Tuffy in background

The author Tom Douglas at age 10 in the front yard of
his new Wawa home after moving from Sinterville

Chapter Thirteen
HOT POTATO BOOGIE

S hirley Kelly tossed me a hot potato, and I handed over my heart.

I had never before experienced such a tumble of sensations. The heady smell of steaming, succulent flesh. Skin black as coal dust and sizzling to the touch. A hiss of pent-up intensity at the first thrust of my probing fingers. The exquisite burst of exotic flavours as I took the soft, white, inner flesh into my mouth.

That potato sure beat the grease-coated home fries my mother served at almost every meal.

Some fellows remember, right down to the spearmint taste of her gum, the first time they ever kissed a girl. Others have fond memories of finally getting up enough nerve to hold hands at the roller rink.

I first fell seriously, head-over-heels in love the night Shirley reached into the front pockets of her jeans and pulled out a potato in each hand.

Gathering up twigs, birchbark, and small branches from beneath the trees hiding us from the rest of humanity, she next produced a kitchen match from her pocket, scraped it against a nearby rock, and soon had a small bonfire blazing.

At my age, I wasn't even allowed to touch the cardboard matchbox my dad kept next to the space heater in our living room, let alone take a match from it. A frisson of unfamiliar depravity coursed through me as a realized I was in the company of a girl who really knew her way around.

Even more enthralling, she had to be at least eleven or twelve years old, a member of the "wild" Kelly family that lived just outside town and was always getting into some sort of trouble that kept tongues wagging from one end of Wawa to the other.

What had I done to fall into the clutches of this older woman? Well, for starters, I was the only one in our group to answer "I would" when she asked who'd like to go out in the bush and play pioneer. I didn't know what a pioneer was, but it had to be more fun than catching lightning bugs in a Mason jar, which was what I'd been doing with my brother Greg and a couple of other guys when Shirley wandered by.

With Greg's whiny voice ringing in my ears that he was going to tell Maw, Shirley and I headed for the stand of timber out behind our house, while my erstwhile companions raced home to spread the news of my wicked downfall. I might end up getting whacked with the big stick my mother kept handy to hoist clothes out of the boiling water in her ancient washing machine, but something told me it would be well worth it.

And it was. Over the years, I have dined on baked potatoes smothered in sour cream and sprinkled with caviar in the Queen's Grill aboard the luxurious Queen Elizabeth 2 as the mighty ocean liner plied its way to Europe across the North Atlantic. I have delighted in that first, crunchy bite of *patate frite* in a Parisian brasserie. And I have gorged myself on the tangy *kartofflen* they serve with sauerkraut and sausage at the Munich Oktoberfest.

But I have never tasted anything as mouthwateringly memorable as the charcoal-blistered potato Shirley served me on a stick in the wilds of Wawa that summer night more than half a century ago.

No salt and pepper. No butter. No fancy foil jacket. Just an ash-covered tuber she'd tossed into the fire and baked while we waited, scratching our blackfly bites and talking about the Wild Bill Elliot movie we'd seen the Saturday before at the Lions Club hall.

A girl who liked Wild Bill Elliot and could cook like she could? I was sure I'd found my life's companion.

But it wasn't to be. Perhaps I committed some unpardonable faux pas by letting her stomp out the embers of our makeshift campfire all by herself while I gnawed at the last morsel of my first *pomme de terre au grit*. Or maybe I broke some law of the frontier by cutting short our stint as pioneers, allowing as how it was getting dark and I had to get home before I got a real licking.

Anyway, from then on, despite several clumsy attempts on my part to entice Shirley back into the woods in a futile effort to recapture that magic day, I didn't seem to exist anymore when she was around. Gerry Johnson whispered to a gaggle of his friends that he'd played pioneer with Shirley, and the story session broke up with dirty little-boy snickers and mocking glances in my direction.

I think the whole thing ran its course in a week or so and that would have been the end of it, except for the fact that fate had one more dirty trick to play on me.

The following Friday night, my mother and father were preparing to stroll down the street to the Carter place, where they enjoyed a weekly round-robin cribbage tournament. Even though I argued I was old enough to look after the household while they were gone, my parents still insisted that one of the older neighbourhood kids stay with us for the couple of hours they'd be out socializing.

"That must be the new babysitter now," my mother called from her bedroom as she touched up her lipstick. "Would you please let her in, Tommy?"

When I replay the scene in my mind, I endow the Tommy Douglas of those days with a strong feeling of premonition, as though sensing that something was about to happen that would come as a real shock.

But that's probably been added in the editing room because I can't think of any signs that would have given me warning. New babysitters were common at our house. We went through them like chunks of ice from the blockhouse on a hot summer's day.

At any rate, I did my mother's bidding, and to paraphrase an old expression, love flew out the window the minute Shirley Kelly walked through the door.

Chapter Fourteen

UNCLE HARRY FLIPS HIS WIG

Being the oldest son in a family where the father had traded in his World War II uniform and many of his paternal duties for a multi-year membership in the John Barleycorn Overachievers Club, I found a lot of responsibilities landing on my shoulders.

Some were less onerous than others. For instance, collecting the mail from the Wawa general store that also served as the town post office was something to look forward to. The owner, a kindly man, always had some new confection he wanted you to sample to see if you thought it would be a big seller.

It was years before it finally dawned on me that he'd already bought that season's supply of the commodity, and one small boy's opinion as to its marketability would have been not only much too little but also far too late.

Anyway, among the Christmas cards and "Third and Final" notices I picked up one early December day was a letter addressed in a familiar scrawl to Mrs. Dorene Douglas. Reading the envelope, I bit clean through the stem of the licorice pipe Mr. Bernardo had asked me to test market. First of all, other than a baby bonus, I'd never seen any mail addressed to my mother before—at least, not since my father had come home. Secondly, I wondered why my rich uncle Harry would be writing her a letter.

Well, he wasn't exactly my uncle, he was my great uncle, having married my dad's father's sister. But he wouldn't let any of us kids call him Great Uncle Harry. "When you weigh over three hundred pounds," he'd say with a booming laugh, "you don't need to draw any unnecessary attention to it." Not that he was particularly fat. Several of Wawa's hardrock miners had suggested so at one time or another and had wakened up wondering what freight train had hit them. He was big, and he had a quick temper, but he could also be the nicest man in the world, if you didn't cross him.

Years later, while surfing the channels on late-night television, I came across an image of Burl Ives that gave me pause. The folk singer was playing Big Daddy to Elizabeth Taylor's Maggie in the Hollywood version of *Cat on a Hot Tin Roof*. I sat mesmerized for the next hour or so because the relationship between those two was hauntingly reminiscent of the affectionate exchanges I'd witnessed time and again between my mother and Uncle Harry.

He openly adored her. A mountain of a man, and bald as the proverbial billiard ball, he harboured no illusions about a young, strikingly pretty woman being romantically attracted to him. He simply liked her and got a kick out of her off-the-wall humour.

He called her "Sugar" and laughed uproariously at the zingers she'd fire at him whenever he and his wife came to call—which wasn't often because they lived in Sault Ste. Marie, an exhausting ten-hour train ride away.

Uncle Harry was a big man in more ways than one.

Realizing that our family was struggling to make ends meet on my father's meagre salary, Harry and his wife Marguerite would ship a box of toys up to us every Christmas to augment the ring of gifts under the tree. Unfortunately, for all their generosity, they had no children of their own and had no idea what kids liked. One year they gave me a copy of George Orwell's *1984*. I think I was seven at the time. And they had terrible memories for names and genders. The year I was nine I got a musical top and my four-year-old brother got the set of Roy Rogers six-guns I'd been coveting.

That's how I recognized the handwriting on the envelope addressed to my mother. Uncle Harry was like a big kid at Christmas and took personal pride in addressing each of the gift labels himself—much to our bewilderment when the present didn't suit the recipient. No one can ever imagine what persuasive powers it took for me to trade that musical top for my brother's six-guns. I made threats and broke promises that are probably chiselled in capital letters on some celestial scoreboard somewhere.

I held back the suspicious letter when I got home after school that day, handing over the rest of the packet and eyeballing my mother as though I were the movie detective Philip Marlowe waiting for her to trip herself up. And she did.

"Is that all there was, Tommy?" she asked with concern, after quickly flipping through the sheaf of envelopes several times. Mail delivery to Wawa was erratic, especially at Christmas, when the postal clerk got forgetful after making his round of commercial deliveries to merchants with a bottle of Yuletide cheer under their counters.

"That's all," I replied, then after a dramatic pause added with a flourish. "Unless you were looking for...this."

She snatched the envelope from my outstretched hand

and tore it open, sighing with relief when two slips of paper, one white and one blue, fluttered to the floor. Before she could retrieve them, I scooped them both up, scanned them quickly and uttered something profound like "Aha!"

The blue piece of paper was a cheque made out to my mother for the sum of twenty dollars, a sizeable amount in those days. The white notepaper contained one word in Uncle Harry's handwriting: "Shush!"

I had expected a guilty confession from the suspect. Perhaps a pleading request to keep this our secret. Or a quick admonition for me to mind my own business as she stuffed the incriminating evidence down the front of her blouse. What I hadn't anticipated was for her to burst out laughing and to comment about the accusing scowl on my face.

She was still erupting into snippets of mirth when my father came home from work a few minutes later, and she showed him the mail that I'd brought home. Every bit of it—including what I'd come to think of as Uncle Harry's extortion payment. For some reason, both parents had a good laugh when she explained how dramatically I'd handed over the one envelope.

Over dinner—while my younger brother drank his milk out of the Jungle Jim bamboo mug he'd received from our benefactor the previous Christmas, when I'd been given a Snow White tea set—my dad explained that Uncle Harry sent my mother a cheque for twenty dollars each year to buy herself something special. He got a big kick out of believing it was a secret shared between the two of them and, since money really was tight, my folks went along with it and no one got hurt in the process. The windfall went towards defraying the inevitable extra costs of Christmas.

Just how much my mother's opinion of him mattered to Harry was demonstrated one time when he and his wife made a surprise trip up the Algoma Central Railway line to our little village. They took a taxi from the train station, and my parents had only a minute or so from the time the cab stopped in front of our house until the guests were at the door to warn us not to say anything about Uncle Harry's new hairpiece.

Sure enough, he came through the door with a proud smile on his face and an elaborate wig on his previously bald head. One stern look from my dad was all it took to stifle any childish giggles that had been about to break forth.

The meal went off without a hitch, but Uncle Harry became increasingly agitated as no one mentioned the full head of hair perched on his dome. Finally, he couldn't stand it any longer.

"That was an excellent dinner, Sugar," he said, sipping from a glass of the wine he'd brought with him. "But tell me something. Do you notice anything different about me?"

"Yes, I do, Harry," said my mother with a straight face as she began clearing the dishes away in preparation for dessert.

"Well, what do you think?" he asked expectantly.

Mother paused in the midst of retrieving a plate from the table and gave him a matter-of-fact look. "Do you really want to know?"

Uncle Harry's short fuse was legendary, and I think my mother was having second thoughts about telling him the honest truth.

"Yes, I really want to know," he replied with a beatific smile. If a three-hundred-pound ex-lumberjack can preen, he preened.

"Well, quite frankly," my mother said after a few seconds, "you look like Paul Bunyan in a coonskin cap."

Aunt Marguerite choked on the wine she was sipping. My

dad slowly put down the dinner napkin he'd been using to dab at his lower lip. I think I actually felt the hair rise on the nape of my neck. All eyes were on Uncle Harry.

Without missing a beat, he reached up, whipped off the wig, and flipped it into the corner of the room. "Well, Mel," he said, turning to my dad, "what do you think of those Maple Leafs? Aren't they having a great year? Do you think they'll beat the Red Wings tomorrow night?"

There followed a communal sigh of relief, and the involuntary tableau that had formed around the dinner table jerked back into real time. As always, Mother's dessert was a great success. Uncle Harry—as special guest—overruled my parents and let us kids feel grown up by having a little coffee in our milk. The singsong around the piano elevated gusto to new heights, and three sleepy kids went to bed with a crisp one-dollar bill tucked into their pyjama pockets.

The visitors had an early train to catch and were gone when we youngsters woke up the next morning. Like a posse closing in on Billy the Kid's hideout, we raced to the corner of the living room where Paul Bunyan's coonskin had been hurled the night before.

It was gone—and to the best of my knowledge, Uncle Harry never wore, nor even mentioned, the hairpiece again.

Chapter Fifteen
FLIRTATIONS IN A SNOW BANK

All kids think their mothers look like movie stars. The difference in my case is that mine really did!

If you're old enough—or if you're a late-night movie buff—picture a young Barbara Hale, who later played Della Street to Raymond Burr's Perry Mason. Now shade in a little sultriness à la Ava Gardner and you come close.

Add the zaniness of Lucille Ball and the irreverent wit of Carole Lombard and you'll understand why grown men used to make fools of themselves just to be around her. She'd kid them unmercifully, and they'd lap it up.

My mother had a sixth sense for those who enjoyed her put-downs as well as for those who might be devastated by them. She never picked on anyone who couldn't take it, and she never picked on anyone at all unless they fired the first salvo.

If she had one fault in this regard, it was that she wasn't able to differentiate between those who considered her attention harmless fun and those who took it as a kind of offbeat flirtation. On more than one occasion, so the story goes, my long-suffering dad had to straighten out—sometimes literally—an overzealous, would-be playmate who mistook my mother's good-natured jibes for verbal love darts.

There was the time, for instance, when a Sinterville neighbour offered to drive my mother home from a party where my father was having too good a time singing ribald war songs with some new-found buddies. It was the middle of winter, and much too far for her to walk home alone.

She accepted the ride, only to realize to her intense discomfort a few minutes later that the neighbour had headed down a little-used mining road. To make matters worse, he kept repeating in a drunken slur how much he loved her and rejoicing at the fact that in just a few minutes they would be alone at last.

Alone was what my mother soon became as the car slid into a ditch and her enthusiastic admirer began snoring loudly with his forehead resting on the steering wheel. Anyone who has survived a northern winter will tell you that you are never more alone than when sitting in a stalled car in the middle of nowhere with your fingers and toes beginning to freeze.

After pleading and prodding got no response, my mother finally roused the sleeping Lothario by shoving handfuls of snow down the neck of his shirt. She didn't know how to drive a car, so she got out and pushed while her shivering suitor tried to rock the vehicle out of the ditch by gunning the motor at erratic intervals.

And that's the scene my father and an OPP officer came upon a few minutes later as they drove up in the town's lone police cruiser. Someone at the party had reported seeing my mother and her tipsy escort leave, and my dad—his emotions lurching swiftly from boozy indifference to intense jealousy—headed for the cop shop to organize a two-man posse.

Once the search party had established that my mother wasn't at home—there were no home telephones in the village, so it meant driving there—they proceeded down the few roads that were kept open in winter until they spotted tire tracks weaving from ditch to ditch and followed them.

Sad to relate, those were less than enlightened times, and since the foiled philanderer was half native Canadian, the OPP officer suggested that he'd wait in the cruiser with my mother while my dad taught the "halfbreed" a lesson.

To my father's credit, he turned down the offer, and that was the end of it. I heard all about it the next day when I was doing a jigsaw puzzle in the living room, and my mother and her best friend were in the kitchen having a coffee. Adults tend to forget that kids have pretty big ears when it comes to gossip. It didn't bother or surprise me that somebody had made a pass at my mother. She was a "fine-looking woman" as Uncle Harry used to tell her. But I couldn't understand the part about the "halfbreed."

I let a couple of days go by and then asked my mother what the word meant. She gave me a funny look, wondering, I guess, how much of the story I had heard. Then she sighed and explained to me that some people tended to look down on others who had mixed blood in their veins. That confused me all the more.

"But you told me your family came from Ireland and Dad's came from Scotland," I pointed out. "Does that make us halfbreeds?"

For some reason, my mother found this funny. "I guess it does," she said with a chuckle. "But somehow the word has taken on a bad meaning and we shouldn't use it. Promise me you won't, okay?"

Heck, compared to all the difficult promises she asked me to keep, that one was easy. Much easier than promising never again to tie my brother Greg to a tree when he wouldn't stop following me and my friends around.

Chapter Sixteen
SHOCK TREATMENT

D ad's drinking problem, despite his efforts to cut down, continued to be a source of anxiety for all of us. He wasn't mean. He never beat us when he was on a binge. My brothers and I always had a roof over our heads, food in our bellies, and clothing to wear. When Dad was sober, he was as kind, mild-mannered, and gentlemanly as anyone on earth. But when "just one beer before supper" turned into three or four, we braced ourselves for what was to come. The pattern hardly ever varied.

First, he'd become sentimental. He'd sit at the piano and play tender love songs for our mother, Dorene—or Dodie as he affectionately called her in that mellow period between the first sip of good cheer and that last, fateful swallow from Dr. Jekyll's test tube. Wartime love songs like "We'll Meet Again," "Long Ago and Far Away," and "Kiss Me Once" would degenerate into half-forgotten army ditties that got more ribald with the downing of each beer. Eventually he'd succumb grudgingly to our mother's increasingly stern warnings to "stop that nonsense in front of the kids."

He'd retreat into the kitchen, and we'd cringe at the sound of the cupboard door opening. That's where he kept his perpetual bottle of Old Porch Climber. A couple of belts of that whiskey while he grumbled at the kitchen table, becoming more and more incoherent, and then the snoring would begin that signalled his slide into oblivion.

We kids marvelled at how he could sprawl unconscious on a kitchen chair without toppling over. We'd learned early on not to disturb him or try to get him to go to bed. While he never got physically violent, he could tear a young ego to shreds with vile insults that called into account every one of your shortcomings, including several you'd hoped nobody had noticed, and a few you'd never even thought of yourself.

We'd leave him sitting there, occasionally muttering in his sleep as he revisited real and imagined slurs, and get ourselves ready for bed. Whenever we'd ask our mother what was wrong with Daddy, she'd tell us he'd had a hard day at the office or had heard some bad news. As the years passed, we figured he must have received more bad news than that Job character we learned about at Sunday School.

And those were the good nights.

Sometimes he wouldn't come home at all. Our mother would start preparing supper around five o'clock, so everything would be out of the way in time for us to tune in to the evening radio programs beamed in from Sault Ste. Marie— that long-lamented metropolis of 30,000 souls some 150 miles to the south of us in the land of civilization.

As each bus from the Helen Mine trundled down our street without stopping in front of our house, Maw would become increasingly agitated. Neglected pots would boil over, or she'd nick herself with a paring knife, as she glanced more and more often at the ticking clock above the stove.

Even now, as I think back to those times, a feeling of

cold dread creeps over me, starting in my fingers and toes and seeping slowly into the pit of my stomach. I have to consciously relax tense muscles and force myself to take long, deep breaths.

Supper on those fatherless evenings consisted of slightly burned comestibles served with empty cheerfulness on Maw's part as she tried to deflect our questions by talking about the upcoming Christmas concert, or school field day, or whatever. Every once in a while she'd dab at her eyes and blow her nose, suggesting with a sheepish smile that another cold must be coming on, but she didn't fool anybody.

If it was wintertime, she'd have to put on Dad's parka and a pair of boots after clearing the supper dishes. Then it was out to the run-down shack behind the house to fill up and lug in the can of fuel oil for the space heater in the living room.

I used to yearn for the sour smell of stale beer in the house the morning after one of Dad's absences. This meant that at least he'd made it home and was sleeping it off on the living room couch. Otherwise, he'd be gone for two or three days, and the household would take on the chilled atmosphere of a death-row vigil as we waited for some sign that he was alive and well.

Like many heavy drinkers, Dad was canny enough to time his binges in such a way that they rarely jeopardized his job. Friday nights you could make book on the fact that he wouldn't be home. If he was still AWOL Monday morning, Maw would get word to his superiors that he was ailing. He usually had enough sense to come rolling in Monday evening so that he could make it to work Tuesday morning, hung over but able to coast through the day. Holiday weekends extended this routine by twenty-four hours.

I don't know for sure, but I suspect the company turned a blind eye to a lot of the drinking that went on in those post-war years because many of the employees were returned veterans with alcoholic tendencies—to put it kindly. I'm not suggesting that this was an act of grateful compassion on the part of management. Rather, if they'd fired everyone who missed work because of a drinking problem, they'd have been forced to go down into the mines themselves. And it was easier to forgive the occasional indiscretion than to try to recruit people stupid or desperate enough to move to an area that had a widespread reputation as a mudhole infested with blackflies and mosquitoes, where the highlight of the social season was the mine employees' five-pin bowling banquet.

I remember one incident during the period we later referred to as "The Exodus That Never Was," when we witnessed Dad run the gamut of crazed emotions from enraged madman to heartbroken swain.

My brothers and I were in bed asleep one night when we awoke with a start to the sound of shouting and pounding just outside our bedroom door. Sinterville's two-bedroom bungalows—little more than haphazardly insulated shacks—were so small and cramped that one wag once suggested that even the mice had to take a number to line up at the mousetrap.

What we were hearing that scary, scary night were Dad's howls of drunken outrage as he banged on the door to the matrimonial bedroom next to our three-kid dormitory. He'd been missing for about thirty-six hours, which he considered no more serious than going to the corner store for cigarettes, and couldn't understand why Maw had barricaded herself in their bedroom.

When pounding with the side of his fist didn't do the job, Dad resorted to kicking in the bottom panel of the door. This brought all three of us kids out of our own room, shrieking for him to leave our mother alone.

Like an enraged bear, Dad turned his attentions from the splintered door and began a verbal assault on us—using old army expressions that luckily we were too young to understand, let alone take offence at. But they were enough to bring Maw out of her sanctuary, and the sight of her stopped all four of us in mid-harangue.

She was breathtakingly beautiful, dressed in her Sunday best, her hair newly combed and fresh lipstick on her lips. The fact that it was about four o'clock in the morning threw all of us into a state of confusion, as did the realization that she had a suitcase clutched in her left hand, while the fingers of her right hand slowly worked loose her wedding rings. These she threw at Dad while she shooed us kids back into our bedroom and slammed the door.

Dad stood dumbfounded in the hallway while we followed Maw's hurried instructions to get dressed and to dump the remaining contents of our dresser drawers into the three suitcases she'd taken down from our closet shelf. Before any of us really knew what was happening, we were all standing in the living room, the silence so loud you could actually hear the slow whir of the second hand on the electric clock.

At that point, one of the strangest and most disconcerting things I've ever witnessed happened. Dad started to cry. Great choking sobs. Then he knelt down in front of our mother and begged her not to leave him. He blubbered all sorts of promises, gathering us three kids together as a kind of peace offering.

Before you knew it, all of us were crying—and we kids were pleading with Maw not to leave Daddy. As the weeping and wailing reached a crescendo, Maw broke through the caterwauling with the promise that she'd stay for the time being if we'd all give her some peace and quiet by going to bed.

Dad repaired to the living room couch, and we three kids stumbled back into our bedroom, climbing into bed and staring off into space until fatigue finally overtook us.

The next morning, Maw calmed our anxieties by telling us she and Dad had had a long talk and he'd promised to "get some help," which none of us understood. But the sight of the wedding rings back on Maw's left hand assured us that things had been patched up and that we weren't going to have to leave for parts unknown.

For a while, strange men came to the house to engage Dad in long, quiet discussions that we never got to hear because we were always told to go outside and play. He attended meetings on a fairly regular basis, and weeks went by without any more incidents.

But Christmas came around and Dad allowed as how he could handle a drink or two without any problem. One or two at Christmas became three or four at New Year, and before long the old routine had begun once more.

But nothing as terrifyingly dramatic as that living room ultimatum ever happened again. And I never again saw my dad cry—until the day of my mother's funeral, almost four decades later.

Chapter Seventeen

DONNY BERNARDO OWES ME A HERSHEY BAR

I was having trouble figuring out why Donny Bernardo hadn't fallen to the floor, kicking and screaming in agony from the poison eating away at his insides.

Instead he was still standing beside me, a quizzical smile on his face and his open-mouth breathing sending wafts of garlic-scented chocolate my way.

The quizzical smile was the result of an unexpected gift he'd just received from an unbelievable source—me. The garlic-scented chocolate was a combination of the heavily spiced spaghetti his mother had fed him for lunch and the chocolate bar I had handed over to him a few minutes before. The only other thing I'd ever given him was chicken pox, so it was little wonder he found my sudden generosity a bit hard to comprehend.

The fact was, I'd thought the confection was laced with poison, and as the minutes ticked by without Donny doubling up in acute pain, I began to realize I'd been had. There was absolutely nothing wrong with the Hershey Bar I'd been given a short time before by a man I'd seen only once at a party at my parents' place.

Our house was action central almost every Friday and Saturday night. In post-World War II Wawa, a piano player was worth his weight in beer caps. If he also owned the piano, his house became a weekend shrine to fallen comrades, half-suppressed war memories, and the dawning realization among those assembled that the time spent fighting fascism had left them years behind those who'd been smart enough to avoid going overseas at all costs.

I don't know about other houses, but at our place we kids were expected to behave like trained monkeys once the adults grew bored belting out the same war ditties they'd sung a thousand times or more. We were paraded in front of the company and expected to sing songs we'd learned by rote: "Bless This House," "Her Golden Hair Was Hangin' Down Her Back," "Just A'Wearyin' For You," and other crowd pleasers my dad pounded out on our cigarette-scarred, beer-stained, out-of-tune piano.

I wax nostalgic when I think of those songs now, but at the time it was terrifying to be trooped out in front of a bunch of inebriated strangers in our living room and told to perform. Nobody beat us if we didn't, but then nobody had to. We always sang our little hearts out because it was expected of us. Somewhere along the line it had been ingrained in us that you did what the grown-ups told you to do. Without question.

And that's how I found myself in the Lions Club hall one Saturday afternoon, hoping Donny wouldn't keel over until the lights were turned off and the weekly installment of *Don Winslow of the Navy* started to play, slightly out of sync, on the large screen set up at the front of the room. If my poison-laden pal swooned too soon, they'd probably cancel

the one-time-only showing of the Saturday afternoon fare
and find some excuse not to give us back our quarters.

It must be hard for young people to imagine, in a world
with videos on demand, iPods, and such, that there ever was
a time when these didn't exist. And it probably boggles their
minds to be told that all Wawa laid claim to electronically in
the late 1940s was a single radio signal beamed from Sault
Ste. Marie. On blizzardy winter nights the reception would
consist of radio voices sounding like penguins broadcasting
a fish derby from Antarctica.

That's why the Saturday movies were a community event
in Wawa. The youngsters got their Saturday afternoon serial,
cartoon, and western, and the adults could count on something a little more sophisticated in the evening when *Riders
of the Purple Sage* gave way to *The Dolly Sisters* or *Gaslight*.

Not too many adults ever braved the mayhem of Saturday
afternoon movies Wawa style. There were dogfights—
nobody had ever passed a rule that you couldn't bring
your pet in with you—and every once in a while a whole
row of excited youngsters would over-rock the long bench
they were sharing and fly, ass-over-gumboots, into the row
behind them.

I actually witnessed a scene once where the distraught
Lions Club member who'd volunteered to oversee the afternoon's proceedings got up in front of his raucous charges and
announced that if one more dog peed on the screen, all pets
would be banned from future showings. He immediately
disappeared beneath a hail of half-eaten cheese sandwiches,
empty Dixie cups, chocolate-bar wrappers, apple cores, and
orange peels.

But sometimes there were family movies, like *Bambi* or
National Velvet, that played both the matinee and evening
performances. Such was the case on this particular occasion

when the fellow who'd been at my parents' soirée the night before called me over to where he was seated and asked me to sing the song he'd heard me perform.

He was sitting with another man, who had not been at the Friday night gathering, and the family friend raved about what a great little singer I was. At that point, I was uncomfortable at being asked to sing. My mother's warnings about not talking to strangers were in conflict with my father's boozy insistence that you perform on command.

The proffered Hershey Bar did nothing to persuade me to burst forth in song. In the first place, chocolate bars had been in short supply during the war years and I'd never seen one like this. Furthermore, I was convinced that this suspiciously friendly adult manufactured the contents and wrappers in some cobwebbed lab and used them to poison children. I have no idea why I thought this.

Finally, I decided that the safest strategy would be to sing the song at top speed and then cut and run for the other side of the hall, which to an imaginative youngster's mind was like escaping to Australia.

Everything worked according to plan until I looked down and saw the Hershey Bar sticking out of my shirt pocket where my persistent benefactor had tucked it after my rapid rendition of "Mairsy Dotes."

Donny spotted the booty at the exact same moment and began hollering "dibs" on his share of the prize. Certain that the first bite would result in instantaneous death, I allowed as how I wasn't hungry and handed over the brown-and-silver-papered treat.

It disappeared in one gulp, paper and tinfoil flying through the air and settling around my companion's running-shoed feet. My deathwatch lasted through the screenings of chapter twelve of the serial, a *Little Lulu* cartoon, and an entire

Our Gang comedy feature.

There were no death rattles from Donny. All I heard above the uneven soundtrack was the soft rasp of his breathing and the occasional gurgle from his stomach as it merrily digested the unexpected candy.

When the afternoon's entertainment ended, my companion rubbed his eyes with his index knuckles, belched happily, and said he'd see me at school on Monday.

From that day forward, I never spoke to Donny Bernardo again after the way he tricked me into giving him a perfectly good Hershey Bar and never even had the courtesy to offer me one bite!

Chapter Eighteen
THE HARPER TOUCH

H er face haunts me to this day.
Melody Harper.

Eyes flat and expressionless. A mouth as set and stern as those you see in old photographs of pioneer women slumped wearily outside their sod huts.

An emaciated body clad in hand-me-downs that looked as though they hadn't been within spitting distance of soap and water in recent memory.

And a head of tangled hair that very likely served as home to more than one species of six-legged critter.

Melody was several years older than me. She was in Grade Seven or Eight and must have been around twelve, although she had a weary resignation to her that put her well beyond her years.

Melody Harper. What kind of magnificent plans had someone had for a new-born infant pretty enough to be named Melody? Were there music lessons in the offing? Or ballet? Did the name-giver hope the little girl would grow up to be a famous actress? A country-and-western singer perhaps?

Anyway, things didn't go according to plan, at least for the short while that Melody and I shared time and space together. In the caste system that existed in any schoolyard I ever played in, Melody was a leper. She was one of "those Harper people" who lived in a tarpaper shack out in the woods somewhere. She and half a dozen brothers and sisters attended our school, but none of them said very much.

In fact, you couldn't even get a rise out of them when you brushed up against one of them and then placed your hand on the next person you met, whispering ominously, "You've got the Harper Touch!"

This ritual would cause the "infected" party to shudder, swipe a hand over the part of his or her body now contaminated in such a vile way, and race to the next victim, offloading the "Harper Touch" and whispering the curse.

If the mean streak was wide enough in the collection of vile little creatures standing around the schoolyard when the game got started, it could last all the way through recess.

To my everlasting regret, I have to admit I played the game. At the time, it seemed like innocent fun. Nobody actually got harmed by it, and besides, you were afraid that if you didn't play, the rules would be changed and people would start cringing away from being infected with something revolting that bore your name.

Talk about children's playgrounds being microcosms of global societies. At that time, we were little more than a decade and an ocean removed from Kristalnacht, jackboots, yellow Stars of David, and the Final Solution.

But we were only kids, the apologist within me insists. We didn't really know we were hurting anyone's feelings. And yet I can still see all the Harpers running to one end of the schoolyard when the game began, the younger ones huddling behind the older ones, who faced outward like musk oxen defending their herd against predators.

As usual, the game was played right under the noses of the teachers who were supposed to be supervising us, but were unaware of what was going on. The kids were playing tag and that kept them out of trouble, so leave well alone seemed to be the order of the day.

The inevitable, however, finally happened. One day, during that restless, volatile last week before summer holidays, the youngest—and thus the least hardened—Harper, a little girl in Grade One, broke into tears at the razzing she was taking. The newest—and thus the least hardened—teacher heard her tale of woe with increasing outrage.

The matter must have been discussed at a hurried staff meeting because orders came down from on high—the principal's office—that the next person who uttered the curse would be called up in front of the entire school and given the strap—a long strip of rubberized canvas the principal always carried with him in his back pocket.

Like so many acts of legislation that are passed to punish the guilty and end up damaging the innocent, the principal's edict backfired.

What happened was that Melody Harper, responding to whatever demons had been eating away at her throughout the eight years she'd attended the school, chose the hushed moment just before the principal declared the school closed for the summer holidays to make her stand.

Like Ike addressing his troops before Operation Overlord, our fatuous principal had lined us all up in the schoolyard, row upon row, where he could make his farewell address to a captive audience.

He'd just finished and was taking a deep breath to make his long-awaited announcement, when Melody reached out to the girl in the next row and in a stage whisper that could be heard from one end of the schoolyard to the other announced, "You've got the Harper Touch."

A smart man would have ignored the remark, quickly announced year's end and let the incident lie trampled in the dust raised by sixty excited youngsters heading for home.

But our principal was not a smart man. "Who said that?" he barked, then blanched when Melody disdainfully raised her offending hand.

I wish I were making this all up, but anyone who was there that day will confirm that Wawa's answer to Ichabod Crane called Melody to the front of the assembly, muttered something about rules being rules, and administered several teeth-clenching blows of the "Black Doctor" as he so cutely referred to his strap whenever he pulled it out to threaten the inmates. As young as we were, we all knew there was some-thing sick about the way he fondled the thing.

I still remember, with admiration and a certain amount of self-recrimination, what the disdainfully cool and collected Melody muttered in a loud aside as she ambled slowly back to her place in line that day, "Now *he's* got the Harper Touch."

Either not hearing, or choosing to ignore that remark, the principal turned embarrassed silence into pandemonium by announcing the holiday.

Melody entered high school that fall, and I never heard anything about her after that. But I think of her from time to time, always with the fervent hope that the Harper Touch turned out to have magical properties that somewhere, somehow turned her life into a beautiful song.

Chapter Nineteen

ALL I WANT FOR CHRISTMAS

Butterflies were making nosedives into the pit of my stomach and lying there in a lump. The guffaws from tipsy male members of the audience—who had been dragged to the concert by their long-suffering wives—had just subsided. Grade Seven student Barbara Wilcox, apparently at a loss as to why hoots of laughter had erupted when she recited the line, "Where squirrels hide their nuts in grass," was just finishing her recitation of William Henry Davies poem "Leisure." That meant I was up next.

I loved Christmas as much as the next kid. But I hated Christmas concerts. Around the beginning of December, the concert organizers would contact my father and ask him if he and I would grace them with our presence again that year. Dad would accept the invitation without consulting me. He got a kick out of playing the piano in public, and it never occurred to him that my command performance, singing whatever ditty he picked out, was equivalent to Charles Starrett in the movie *North of the Yukon* having to run a gauntlet of Mounties with whips when he was drummed out of the Northwest Mounted Police. That movie had played the previous Saturday at the Lions Club hall—the same hall where the Christmas concerts were held.

Unlike my dad, I hated appearing at these gong shows. I had nightmares for weeks in advance about forgetting the lyrics to the complicated songs it fell to me to screech out in my prepubescent falsetto. But just like the joke I was to hear years later, I couldn't quit because I was a star.

Not that it took much to be considered a star in post-World War II Wawa. Movies were a weekly affair, television didn't exist, and radio reception was so spotty that listeners played a kind of airwaves roulette to see whether they could enjoy an entire program before the inevitable static started its fingernails-on-the-blackboard interruption.

As an indication of how starved the Wawanauts of those bygone days were for entertainment, the most perennially popular act at Christmas concerts was a shoulder-arms drill by the Grade Eight boys, set to some jingoistic American military march played offstage on a scratchy record. When the boys ended their display by twirling their wooden rifles over their heads—invariably knocking a couple of plumed shakos off in the process—it never failed to get a standing ovation.

My first shot at stardom Wawa-style wasn't so bad. In Grade Two, our teacher, Miss Grexton, made me an offer I couldn't refuse. She knew I had a crush on Ginny Haynes by the fawning looks and occasional passed notes—although you couldn't express your undying ardour that well when the only sentences you'd learned to put together at that point were "See Spot run" and "Look at Baby Sally." Anyway I jumped at the chance when Miss Grexton suggested that at the upcoming Christmas concert Ginny and I should sing the song we'd learned in class, "I'll Give to You a Paper of Pins."

Miss Grexton must have had a secret desire to produce musical comedy because she really got into the role, suggesting that Ginny should be dressed as an English peasant girl and that I should be a "gentleman," decked out in top hat and tails.

There were no costume shops in the Wawa of the mid-1940s, and I doubt there are any there even today. So that meant it fell to our proud and devoted mothers to come up with something that passed for the kind of get-ups our stage-struck teacher had in mind. Although I don't remember exactly, I'm sure Ginny looked properly fetching in whatever rustic garb her mother was able to put together for her, but in retrospect I think I must have looked like Digger O'Dell, the Friendly Undertaker, once my mother was through with her wardrobe assignment. A white shirt, black bow tie, black pants, and a black coat sweater with two strips of ebony-dyed cheesecloth sewn onto the back hemline to make a tailcoat were fairly easy to come up with. But where in blazes was she supposed to find a top hat?

My mother was nothing if not imaginative, so inspiration soon struck. Baby brother Norm, who had made his unscheduled—as far as I was concerned—arrival the previous November, had just graduated to semi-solid food and was gobbling down Pablum, the just-add-milk baby cereal that to me tasted like sweetened, lukewarm sand, as fast as my mother could shovel it into his mouth. An empty Pablum box was readily available. At that time, the dried cereal came in a tall, round box, which served as the crown of the hat. But it had to be black, and this was in the days before felt marking pens, so it took several layers of laboriously applied black Peacock crayon to cover over the blue and yellow printing on the container. A circle of black cardboard was taped to the opening of the box to form the hat's brim. Then my mother cut an elastic band and stapled the ends to either side of the brim to make an invisible chinstrap to keep the contraption on my head. My costume now complete, I was ready for my debut on the Wawa stage.

Our act lasted only a couple of minutes, but I was hooked on showbiz at the end of it when I made a courtly bow to Ginny, who was sitting pretty on a stool in front of me, and the elastic broke on my hat, sending it tumbling into her lap. The roar of laughter and the sound of appreciative applause had me thinking that perhaps I had found my life's calling.

But the subsequent spring concert, which I'd looked forward to with great enthusiasm, didn't turn out so well. Miss Grexton came up with another blockbuster idea by suggesting that my arch rival, Bruce McDermid, and I sing the song "I'm An Old Cowhand," dressed up like Roy Rogers and Gene Autry. For dramatic effect, she told us to unholster our cap guns at the end of the song and shoot off a couple of rounds. But in my haste to outdraw Bruce, I pulled my pistol from its holster with blinding speed, only to watch in horror as the roll of caps fell out of the gun and rolled to the front of the stage. Bruce got the only laugh of that particular gig by aiming his gun at me instead of into the air and firing off a staccato burst of caps at my behind as I bent over to retrieve my ammo.

Crestfallen, I decided that a life in the theatre wasn't for me after all. But I wasn't allowed to quit. My dad had accompanied both duets on the piano and found that he really enjoyed the limelight. When the next Christmas concert rolled around, Miss Grexton had apparently decided that she was a better one-room-school teacher than Broadway impresario and decided not to participate. My dad, though, was ready for his semi-annual brush with fame and volunteered us to perform a father-and-son musical offering, featuring the inspirational anthem "Open the Gates of the Temple." Since I couldn't read music, and the words of the hymn were extremely complicated, I had to learn the whole thing by rote, which took me several weeks of standing by the piano parroting my dad's singing until I knew the whole thing backwards and forwards. I can still rhyme off the words to this day.

Those first hyperactive butterflies started hammering my guts the night of the concert, just before it was our turn to take the stage. I was sure I would forget the lyrics, and I could see Bruce McDermid's leering smile in my mind's eye. But, wonder of wonders, the whole thing went off without a hitch, with Dad at the keyboard and me straining to reach the musical stratosphere on the line "I know that my Redeemer liveth." The lengthy applause at the end of the last chorus convinced my father we should do a run-through of "Her Golden Hair Was Hanging Down Her Back"—the song we had rehearsed as a just-in-case encore. That too was a rousing success, and my fate was sealed. I felt like a deflated balloon after the concert, but my dad had thoroughly enjoyed himself and promised we'd be there same time next year.

Which brings us to that unsettling moment when Barbara Wilcox finished reciting "Leisure" to thunderous applause and it was time for me to follow my dad onstage to wow the gathered throng with a couple of verses of "Bless this House."

Halfway through the performance, my worst nightmare came to pass. I dried. I couldn't remember the next line to save my soul. I stood beside the battered old piano with my mouth open, but nothing would come out. There was a collective intake of breath from the audience as they realized what was happening. But in the best the-show-must-go-on tradition, I turned to my dad and asked him what the next line was. He gave it to me in a loud stage whisper and I managed to finish the hymn without another glitch. Once again, the audience broke into tumultuous applause, and I was congratulated for being a "real trouper" time and again at the post-concert hot chocolate and cookies session that always took place right on stage once the final curtain had come down.

But that was the end of my concert appearances as far as I was concerned, in spite of my father insisting we'd be back with a real tour de force the following spring. It didn't help the next day at school when Bruce McDermid kept up a steady stream of snide remarks about how I'd forgotten the words during my performance.

When the next concert rolled around, I dug in my heels. I would *not* be going on stage and that was that. No litany of paternal threats, pleading, or outright bribery could make me change my mind.

To save face, Dad told everyone that my voice was changing—although that event was really still a couple of years off—and I couldn't hit the high notes any more. Not that I ever could. There was never a mention of concert appearances again, but for many years afterward I couldn't shake the uneasy feeling that my dad had never forgiven me for bringing his musical career, such as it was, to an inglorious end.

Chapter Twenty
WHERE HAVE ALL THE SOLDIERS GONE?

He was introduced to us part way through the first term as Wolfgang. He eventually got over his terror at being amongst strangers in a confusing new homeland, to the point where he could suggest shyly that we call him what his family called him, "Wolfie," which he pronounced "Vulfee."

I can see him in my mind's eye, more than half a century later, almost as clearly as the day our new teacher, Miss Yuzwa, welcomed him to our class. And I still have a cracked and faded class photograph in which Wolfie, by year's end secure enough to let loose, is clowning around by waving at the camera.

But I can't for the life of me remember his last name. And I wish I could because I'd like to see if I could track him down and, if he's still alive, apologize to him for spoiling his first Christmas in his adopted country.

I didn't do it on purpose. It was one of those honest mistakes kids make and perhaps don't think about again for years, if ever. But a Christmas hasn't gone by since I realized my cruel—if innocent—gaffe that I don't utter a silent apology, hoping Wolfie will pick up the signal and understand.

Christmas in post-World War II Wawa was like Christmas in Stalag 17—without the Red Cross parcels. Most of the inhabitants were impoverished war veterans and their families, newly arrived refugees, or alcoholic hardrock miners with few ties to speak of. Money was tight, and even if you had it to spend, the manufacturing plants had not yet retooled from wartime production to the peacetime spewing out of consumer goods.

My mother always managed to squirrel away enough from her household budget to buy inexpensive but thoughtful gifts for me and my two younger brothers. And somehow or other, she also came up with enough to purchase something respectable for me to give to whatever classmate I had drawn at our school Christmas party.

I don't remember whose name I drew that one particular year or what present I might have given, but knowing my mother, it had to be something nice. All I do remember is that Wolfie drew my name, and I wasn't exactly gracious in my acceptance of his gift.

I guess the first jolt of reality hit when Miss Yuzwa read my name off Wolfie's present and handed me a large kitchen matchbox like the ones my dad kept handy to re-light the space heater in our living room when it ran out of fuel in the middle of a sub-zero Wawa night—which happened with annoying regularity.

Everyone else had received gifts wrapped up in Christmas paper, or at least in recycled tissue that Mr. Bernardo had used to cushion the kitchen ornaments he sold at his general store. My present was encased in a red, white, and blue matchbox, my name scrawled boyishly on top with a dull pencil.

If time travel were possible, I would gladly fly back to that last school day before Christmas in the late 1940s and clap a hand over the mouth of the little boy who was my younger self just as I was about to say, "But these aren't even new!"

That would lift the burden, all these years later, of remembering the pained expression that replaced the expectant one on Wolfie's face and his hurt little voice replying, "I did not know you had to give something new!"

Crammed into the matchbox was a platoon of lead soldiers, their painted uniforms chipped, rifles snapped off at mid-barrel, and several with heads or arms missing.

I draw a blank whenever I try to recall what happened after that. I'd like to think that I came to my senses and replied that they were just what I'd been hoping for. On a crasser note, I wish I'd had enough smarts to realize that these were pre-war German toy soldiers that Wolfie had brought with him from overseas and that they'd probably be worth a fortune at some point in the future, even in their dilapidated condition.

But I have no idea what happened to the soldiers...or to Wolfie for that matter. The story ends, in my mind at least, with that plaintive cry from a kid who had endured the horrors of wartime Germany, the indignities of getting settled into a new life in a new land, and the disconcerting reality of having to make new friends and learn new lessons in a language as strange to him as German would have been to me if the fortunes of war had been reversed.

What bothers me most whenever I think about that particular incident is that here was a youngster who'd decided to give up his prize possessions in the spirit of Christmas and ended up being rebuffed for doing so.

It was many years later, after I had had the opportunity to talk to a number of disgruntled veterans from various wars, that I realized the irony of this incident. Just as I had looked with disdain upon a matchbox full of tarnished and battered soldiers, many members of society tend to regard old soldiers as yesterday's heroes who should just fade away once the tumult and the shouting has died. To my way of thinking, old soldiers should be cherished, not discarded.

I hope the ensuing years have been as good to Wolfie as they've been to me. I pray that he soon got over the hurt and confusion caused by my childish insensitivity and that he today enjoys all the good things that life in his adopted homeland can give him.

And I console myself with the thought that perhaps he has somehow come to realize that my initial ingratitude was a fleeting thing and that I eventually became truly thankful for the best of all gifts—the sharing of a personal treasure for all the right reasons.

Chapter Twenty-One
THE HARDER THEY FALL

"**B**ut he's bigger than me!"

I was out of options. My brother Greg had come running into the house crying. He told our mother, while she was drying his tears, that Gerry Johnson had pushed him down. He had a lump on his forehead that was turning a funny purple colour to prove it.

It was a Saturday morning, and our dad had just announced it was noon hour in Halifax. That was his way of saying it was time to open the first beer of the day. He had been trying to cut down on his drinking and, for the most part, he was having some success. But I figured this was one of those days when he had decided to take a little vacation from his good intentions.

I never tired of watching him tip the bottle back to down the contents in one long swallow—a trick I tried one time with a bottle of grape pop and ended up with it all over my shirt front and squirting out my nose. Mission accomplished, Dad took a second bottle out of the refrigerator, saying as he always did that you couldn't fly on one wing. Then he glanced over at me.

"Tommy Boy," he began. He always called me Tommy Boy when he was starting to feel mellow after that first beer. "I want you to find Gerry Johnson and knock his block off." With that, he snapped the cap off his beer and tried to beat his record for downing it without taking the bottle away from his lips.

I was hoping his great thirst would make him forget I was there as he reached for a third beer, with my mother in the background telling him to slow down. He obliged by taking only a small sip from the bottle this time. Then he reached into his shirt pocket and extracted a package of Sweet Caporals, plucking one of the cigarettes out and lighting it with a match he scraped on the underside of the kitchen table. He managed to do all this one-handed, never setting the beer bottle down for a second. That was another thing I enjoyed watching him do.

As he exhaled a long plume of bluish-grey smoke, Dad glanced at me again, looking like he was surprised I was still standing there. "Didn't you hear me?" he asked. "Get out there and beat the crap out of Gerry Johnson."

I suggested that I didn't see why I had to do that. Gerry hadn't done anything to me. Although we were friends, I was scared stiff of Gerry Johnson. He was a head taller than me and one grade ahead of me at school. He could chin himself ten times on the limb of the tree outside his house. He was always doing that to show off to Mary Jane Chrobak, the girl who lived next door to him. I couldn't even reach the tree limb. Not that it mattered because the one time Gerry gave me a boost to reach the branch, I just hung there like a dope. I couldn't even do one chin-up—which Gerry took great delight in pointing out to everybody on the school bus the following Monday.

"Gerry hurt your brother," Dad said, then took another swig of his beer. He obviously thought this was a good enough reason for me to go after Gerry and get the stuffing beaten out of me.

"That's right," I replied. "Gerry hurt Greg. It's up to Greg to get even. I'll go with him."

As soon as the words were out of my mouth, I knew what was coming. "Greg's just a little kid. You're the big brother. It's up to you to fight his battles for him until he's old enough to look after himself."

You're the big brother. I hated that expression. How come they only used it when there was something unpleasant to be done? When there was one slice of our mother's world-famous coconut cream pie left and Dad said he didn't want it, did they say, "Well, you're the big brother. You can have that last piece"? Nope, it was always, "Split the pie with Greg. Cut it in half and let him choose first."

I had to think of something else fast. I could start limping and say I had a big blister on my heel, but I knew that wouldn't work. I had used that excuse last week to get out of helping Dad put the storm windows in the back shed.

I thought about complaining I had a toothache, but they'd probably take me to Doc MacTavish, and he had already almost broken my jaw taking out a tooth with a pair of pliers. The only man who could beat Dad in a beer-drinking contest was Doc MacTavish.

That's when I decided to try to reason with Dad by pointing out that Gerry Johnson was bigger than me.

"The bigger they are, the harder they fall," he replied. That made absolutely no sense to me, but I knew when I was licked. With Greg still whimpering in our mother's lap and Dad lighting up another cigarette, I prepared to meet my doom. I could almost hear the music in the background, like they played when two gunfighters were preparing to meet on the streets of Tombstone.

Then my mother sweetened the pot—an expression my dad used whenever his Legion buddies came over to play poker at our house. She offered to pay me a dollar if I went out there and beat the tar out of Gerry. My head started to spin. I was still afraid of getting hurt, but I was also shocked my mother would want me to "beat the tar" out of anyone. She was such a gentle person herself. However, more than once I had heard her compared to a mother grizzly when her cubs were in danger.

A whole dollar? I used to have to work an entire week collecting grocery orders for Ken Richardson to make that kind of money. A whole dollar would get me into the Saturday movie four weeks in a row. I headed for the front door.

I was hoping against hope that Gerry would realize the error of his ways and apologize to me for pushing my little brother down once he saw me. Or maybe he'd had a sudden appendix attack and was already on his way to Sault Ste. Marie for an operation. Or since it was the summer holidays, he might have left for Toronto or Vancouver, just after pushing Greg, and wouldn't be back for a couple of weeks. Surely Dad would forget all about the incident in a couple of weeks. And I knew my mother would still pay me the dollar, even if all I did was make the effort to track Gerry down.

But this wasn't my lucky day. As I walked slowly down our front steps, I could see Mary Jane Chrobak pushing her baby sister in a buggy, and Gerry was walking along beside her. I decided to turn around and go back into the house, but when I looked through the front door window, there were my parents and Greg peering out at me, waiting for the big fight to start. I could feel my Adam's apple—if I was even old

THE HARDER THEY FALL

enough to have an Adam's apple—bob up and down when I swallowed. My palms were wet, and I was breathing really fast.

"Hey, Mary Jane, look who's here," Gerry said when he spotted me. "It's the great Tommy Douglas, come to fight for his little brother's honour." As usual, Mary Jane giggled. She was the unofficial president of the Gerry Johnson fan club. And the only member as far as I knew.

"You hurt my brother," I said, trying to keep my voice from getting all shaky. "He's just a little kid and you pushed him down."

"He was in our way," replied Gerry, to another giggle from Mary Jane.

"I really think you should apologize to him and tell him it won't happen again," I suggested, trying to avoid the awful moment when Gerry decided to really impress Mary Jane by punching me in the nose.

"I really think you should apologize," Gerry mimicked in a singsong voice. When Mary Jane didn't giggle at this, Gerry turned and looked at her. She giggled on cue. "Your brother's a little suck and your dad's a drunk. And I hear that your mother..."

That's as far as he got. Although I'd heard it used many times, I hadn't really understood what the word "rage" meant until that moment. I ran at Gerry and butted him in the stomach with my head. Somehow we both ended up on the ground, with him on top of me. He started punching me in the face.

I don't like to admit it, but I let John Wayne and Bogie and all my other heroes down right then and there by hollering for help. I yelled for my dad to come to my rescue. "He's killing me!" I shouted. "Somebody stop him."

And then a funny thing happened. I guess I was yelling

so loud that Gerry decided to shut me up. He put a hand over my mouth and I saw my opportunity. I bit down on his baby finger with all my might. Gerry howled and fell off me, giving me the chance to roll over on top of him. Now I was sitting there with a clear shot at his face.

But just as I pulled back my fist to give him a good smack, I felt myself being lifted off him. Somebody had grabbed me under the arms and raised me up into the air. For a moment I thought it was Gerry's father, and I got really mad. But my anger turned to shock when the person who set me down on my feet was my own dad.

"That's enough, Tommy," he said calmly. "Come on back in the house and have a cold drink. We're proud of you."

But Gerry wasn't going to take this lying down. Well, actually, he still was lying down, but he raised himself up on his elbows and said, "He bit me. He didn't fight fair."

"There are no rules in a street fight, kid," my dad replied. Mary Jane giggled, and Gerry scowled at her. I imagined that would be the last time he walked along with her when she was pushing her baby sister in her buggy.

Back home, after Dad had poured me my second glass of ginger ale, I had to ask him the question that was bugging me. "You told me to beat the crap out of Gerry, but as soon as I got my chance, you pulled me off him. Why?"

My dad ruffled my hair and smiled. "I wanted to run out there when he had you down and was punching you in the face. But I figured the odds were that sooner or later you'd get on top. It's better to go out a winner than a loser. Always remember that."

While I could understand the message, it still would have been nice to get in one solid punch before the whole thing was over. Then I had another thought. My mother had promised me a dollar, and it was time to collect.

"No son of mine is going to fight for money," Dad said when I raised the matter. "You fight as a matter of honour, not to make a buck. Knowing that you did the right thing is reward enough."

I knew how important it was to my dad to do the right thing. My mother had told me many times how he volunteered to fight the Nazis even though it meant not only leaving his family but taking a really big cut in pay to do so. Still, I pictured four movies flying away into the distance when I realized I wasn't going to get that dollar.

Then the strangest thing happened. The next day, Dad called me into the back shed and pointed to four cases of empty beer bottles stacked up in the corner. He suggested that maybe I'd like to contact Howard McCabe and collect the one cent a bottle that he paid for empties. Dad added that I could keep the money if I did him this favour. He said his back was acting up, so he didn't think he should take the chance of it getting worse by trying to return the empties to the Legion.

Each case held twenty-four bottles, and there was a paper bag with four more bottles Dad said a neighbour had brought over one night when they were playing cribbage.

I wasn't very good at arithmetic, but it didn't take me long to figure out that when Howard came by to collect the bottles, he would owe me exactly one dollar.

Chapter Twenty-Two
THEY'LL NEVER TAKE MAD DOG ALIVE

I had just taken a bite out of my sandwich when a noise above my head gave me the creeps. I reached slowly for my weapon, dropping the sandwich in the dirt. Jumping to my feet, I aimed my Red Ryder BB gun at the pine tree where the rustling sound had come from.

The intruder cursed me in chipmunk language and scurried along a branch. I lowered my gun, chuckling at myself for being such a scaredy cat. There wasn't another human being for miles around. I was safe here—as I'd known I'd be. That's why I'd picked Dead Man's Drop as my hideout. Sure, I risked a licking for coming up here on my own, but it was a chance I had to take.

Picking up my sandwich from where it had fallen to the ground, I brushed off the pine needles, twigs, and bits of dirt. It was still in pretty good shape, and I was hungry. The climb had left me famished and dying of thirst. I had already drained the last drop of orange pop from the Boy Scout Thermos I'd brought along. I'd have to find a stream soon to refill the Thermos. You could die from sunstroke if you didn't keep your water levels topped up. Bogie had taught me that one.

Actually, Bogie had taught me a lot of things. How to kiss a dame, for instance. I hadn't had a chance to try that one out yet. And how to take a slug to the kisser and not burst into tears. Luckily, I hadn't gone through that one yet either. But I was ready for it. Both of them in fact.

Bogie had been my hero since the days when my dad was overseas. Back in Sault Ste. Marie, Maw had shown an amazing knack for identifying popular tunes. She knew every one of them almost from the first note. That's how she got into the movies free. She'd listen to the radio and when they held the "Name that Tune" contest, she was usually the first one to call in with the right answer. Her prize was a double pass to the movies, and she'd take Aunt Betty and us along with her. Aunt Betty was married to an American GI who was fighting the Japanese, and she was staying with us until it was over.

A movie was the reason I had climbed up the mountain behind our house to take it on the lam until the heat was off. Living in Sinterville, we had to go all the way to Wawa to see a movie at the Lions Club hall. They played a kids' film in the afternoon, but if you hid in the broom closet, you could sneak into the movie they ran for grown-ups after they cleared out all the chocolate bar wrappers, apple cores, orange peels, and sandwich crusts. They didn't sell popcorn, and you had to bring your own grub with you if you wanted to survive through a Tom and Jerry cartoon, a Don Winslow serial, a whole bunch of previews, and a Laurel and Hardy feature.

Last week, I'd managed to sit in the back row where nobody bothered me, and I got to see Humphrey Bogart (funny name for a hero) in *High Sierra*. He played Roy

"Mad Dog" Earle—I memorized the name from the movie poster—and he didn't take any guff from anybody. When he climbed that mountain to avoid the coppers, I cheered out loud and almost got caught sitting there when I should have been on my way home. I had to keep real quiet from then on, even when the cops shot Mad Dog and he fell off the mountain.

That was the previous Saturday, and at school on Monday I was just about to tell my friend Bruce McDermid about my caper when the school bell rang and we had to line up—just like Bogie did in a prison picture I'd seen last winter. The day didn't go so well after that. First of all, Ginny Haynes broke the news that she liked Bruce better than me. Then the bombshell dropped. Doctor MacTavish would be visiting the school on Wednesday to give us all a needle so we wouldn't get scarlet fever.

The whole class groaned at that unwelcome news, but I didn't let out a peep. Nobody had to know that getting needles wasn't my idea of a good time. In fact, I hated getting needles. I'd rather have let Bruce McDermid slug me in the kisser as hard as he could. But Bogie wouldn't let his feelings show and neither would I. However, that didn't mean I was going to take it lying down—or standing up. That's what I told Bruce later, but he didn't see the humour in it. He just bet me I'd react the same way I had that time before when they gave us the shot for mumps, but I told him I had grown up a lot since then. "We'll see," is all he said.

When I woke up two days later and remembered it was Wednesday, I decided I had to come up with a plan real quick. I couldn't let Ginny Haynes see me make a face when they shoved the needle into my arm. Or see me bawl my eyes out like the last time.

Luckily Wednesday was wash day at our house, so my

mother wouldn't be paying too much attention when the school bus came to pick us up and take us to Wawa. I could yell goodbye while she was putting clothes into the washing machine, then make a run for it before the bus arrived.

And that's what I did. Maw had prepared a peanut butter and jam sandwich for me and, while she was putting my younger brother in his playpen, I snuck into the kitchen and filled my Thermos with orange pop from the fridge. I wouldn't be getting the milk they gave us at school, and it was going to be a long, hot, thirsty day.

After the bus had come and gone, I grabbed my BB gun from under my bed and made my way down the back lane, heading for the mountain and Dead Man's Drop, where I knew nobody would be around on a weekday. The last time I had gone there, Gerry Johnson squealed on me, and Dad had given me a few slaps on the behind, telling me never to go there again unless he was with me. But Gerry was on that bus headed for Wawa, so the dirty rat couldn't turn me in this time.

When I got up to Dead Man's Drop, I was worn out from the climb, but I managed to scare the daylights out of myself by peering over the edge of the cliff and seeing the huge rocks down at the bottom. The story goes that they called it Dead Man's Drop because somebody had been killed when they fell from the top and smashed their head on those rocks.

I managed to find a mossy area near some pine trees where I could make my stand. The sun was beating down, and I had forgotten the bottle of Coppertone. It might be mid-September, but you could still get a nasty sunburn, so I made camp under the trees. I wished I'd remembered to bring some comic books to pass the time, but you couldn't have everything.

Boy, it gets boring when you're just sitting in one spot

for a long time. Even though all the pop was long gone, I'd decided not to drink the water in a small pool I found because there were a lot of dead leaves at the bottom and some creepy crawly things floating on top. To quench my thirst, I ate some berries off a bush. No, I wasn't stupid enough to eat a whole bunch at once. I tried a couple and then waited about fifteen minutes to see if they were poison. When nothing happened, I used my ball cap as a basket and picked some more.

Every once in a while I would hear something moving in the trees surrounding me. I'd fire at the sound with my BB gun to keep them pinned down, just like John Wayne would do, but I had to be careful not to run out of ammo. I started to collect some rocks and dead branches to use as emergency weapons if I got attacked, and that made me feel better.

I checked my watch every now and then, but it was amazing how slowly the time was going. It seemed to take the big hand a whole hour just to move from one number to the next. I tried to make things go faster by counting to one hundred, then saying my ABCs backwards, but that big hand still crept along like the turtle in the glass bowl at the back of our classroom.

That thought made me try to imagine what was going on in class at the moment. Doc MacTavish would probably be there with his giant needle that he seemed to enjoy sticking into everybody's arm. I could almost smell the beer on his breath and see his hands shaking as he reached into his bag. I had heard Maw and Dad talking about the doctor's drinking problem one night when they thought I was asleep. I figured if beer didn't agree with him, then he should just stop drinking it or switch to pop. But for some reason he didn't seem to want to do that.

Just then, I started to feel drowsy. I wondered if the berries had been poison after all and I was about to breathe my last gasp. But then I remembered I had talked Gerry Johnson into eating the same kind of berries the last time we were up here, and he was still alive and kicking, so that couldn't be it. Maybe a little nap would do the trick.

When I woke up, I didn't know where I was at first. I was sore all over and my cheek felt funny where I had been lying on the moss. The stuff had seemed soft when I'd first put my head down, but it was like lying on the bare floor with just a blanket under you.

When my head cleared, I looked at my watch again, and I think my hair stood on end just like it does in the cartoons. It was after four o'clock, and the bus would be arriving back from Wawa any minute. My plan had been to stash my BB gun and Thermos under our front porch and be ready to walk in the door when the bus arrived.

I made it down the mountain as fast as I could. My luck was holding. The bus was just coming around the corner as I threw the rifle and canteen under the wooden steps. I might just pull this off yet. If you missed a day at school, our new teacher believed you if you told her the next day you'd been sick. No need to have to pay Howard McCabe to write a note in adult handwriting, like his sister Milly had to do because her teacher didn't trust kids.

For my little trick to work, I had to look like I was coming off the bus, so I crossed the road and waited in the regular drop-off spot. Maw had been out back at the clothesline when I snuck home and hadn't seen me pass by. Bruce McDermid was the first one off the bus and he greeted me with a big grin—which was the first sign that something was wrong. Bruce was never that happy to see me unless he had something to tell me that he knew I wasn't going to like.

And this time was no different. If anything, his smile

got even wider as he delivered the bad news, "If you stayed away from school today so you wouldn't have to get the needle, you wasted your time," he said with glee. "Doctor MacTavish was sick today and didn't come. We're getting our shots tomorrow."

As he walked away laughing, I wondered whether I could make it across the street, retrieve my BB gun, and hit him in the backside before he got to his house.

Chapter Twenty-Three

FREE AT LAST

As I heard it later, Dad decided to tell the big shots at the Helen Mine where they could shove their timeclock the moment he spotted burning logs floating down the Magpie River.

The Wawa of our time was a tiny community, totally surrounded by forested land that the giant lumber companies, like a mutant colony of army ants on a rampage, regularly stripped in ragged sections.

In 1950, the summer before our forced exile in the northern wilderness ended, lightning, careless loggers, or a combination of both started a series of forest fires that eventually ringed the entire town. The good news was that the smell of wood smoke blotted out the perpetual smell of sulphur. The bad news was that thick clouds of wood smoke blanketed the whole area.

The really bad news, however, was that the firefighters were losing the battle against the multitude of conflagrations that threatened to engulf Wawa and everything in it.

Since the highway link to Sault Ste. Marie hadn't yet been

built, there were only two means of exit from that outpost community and back to civilization—by train or by the small pontoon planes that used Wawa Lake as a liquid runway.

As usually happens in dangerous situations, rumours skittered through the community like rats through a warehouse. The rail line out of town had been buried under tons of rubble by a fire-induced landslide. All the pontoon planes were needed to waterbomb the fires—and three of them had already crashed. The water tower had been pumped dry by firefighters and we were all going to die of thirst. The last train to make it into Wawa had delivered a shipment of cyanide pills so that we could all commit suicide rather than face the horror of burning to death.

The one rumour the townspeople chose to believe because it offered a frayed lifeline of hope was that the government had begged, borrowed, and commandeered float planes from all over North America, and they were on their way to Wawa to airlift everybody out.

That uplifting news caused the greatest exodus since a bewigged Charlton Heston took staff in hand and led a cast of film extras across the Mojave Desert. People who could walk, ride a bicycle, flag down one of the few vehicles operating at the time, or harness a farm animal to a wagon began the trek to Wawa Lake, where the air rescue was supposed to take place.

The shores of the lake took on a festive air as people staked out their plot of sand, prepared makeshift beds of clothing and blankets, and started fires to cook whatever rations they'd been able to scrounge up in their haste to get away.

Our family, on the other hand, stayed put in our house. My brother and I would make occasional forays down to the beach and bring back intelligence reports to our mother, but no amount of pleading on our part could get her to budge from our home.

"Your father's at the mine, and when he decides it's time to move down to the lake, we will," was her unshakeable explanation. "Besides, I don't want him running all over the lakeshore looking for us. I said we'd be here until he came for us, and here we'll stay."

What we didn't know at the time was that Dad was frantic with worry. As timekeeper at the mine, he had reports to get out for an upcoming shareholders meeting, and while others were leaving their posts to be with their families, he was told he had to stay on until everything was in order.

From time to time, announcements would come over the loudspeaker in the mine office building that another bus would be leaving shortly to take people home to make preparations for the expected evacuation. Dad kept working at the reports in the hope that he could get them done quickly and be on his way.

At one point, a supervisor walked by and Dad requested permission to pack up and leave. Giving the man what he thought was a reasonable explanation, my father pointed out that his family was at home waiting for him.

"They won't go anywhere without me," he said. "I have to leave now to get them out safely."

"We can't have that, old chap," sniffed the departmental manager, who'd spent World War II as an officer in the reserves, where his worst risk of injury would have been cutting himself on the foil wrapping on a bottle of Johnnie Walker Black. "Duty first, that's our motto here."

At that point, so he told us later, Dad saw burning logs floating down the river outside the office window. It was an indication that the fire was getting dangerously close to the town.

But the words "duty first" served as the trigger that really set dad into action. He'd had a bellyful of duty first ever since he'd been told he wouldn't be returning to Canada after the war, but would remain overseas for another eight months, including another missed Christmas with his family. He slammed shut the ledger he'd been working on and started putting away the items on his desk, ignoring the protests from his supervisor that he couldn't just up and leave.

Reaching the driveway just as a bus was pulling away, Dad managed to flag the vehicle down and arrived at our house in short order. Then, and only then, would our mother agree to gather up as much as we could carry and head for the beach.

The whole thing turned out to be an exercise in futility. There were no planes to evacuate us. That rumour proved as reliable as a politician's campaign promise. But it started to rain the morning after we'd set up camp on the beach. The rain and a shift in the winds extinguished some of the blazes and gave the firefighters a chance to gain control, and we all straggled home to get out of our wet clothes and into a warm bath. The danger eventually passed, and things returned to normal.

For everyone but Dad, that is. He became a non-person at work for disobeying an order, as stupid as the order might have been. Fellow office workers, sensing an imminent execution, gave him a wide berth in the lunchroom and even after hours. While our house had once been action central for parties and celebrations, hardly anyone came around anymore.

As the story goes, one day one of Dad's bosses suggested they go out for a drink after work. Dad pointed out that he was trying very hard to keep his drinking under control. The fellow said one little drink couldn't hurt and assured Dad that he was in the doghouse for the moment, but soon it would all blow over. So Dad relented and went for that one little drink. Which turned into another. And another.

The inevitable happened, as they knew it would. Dad missed work the next day due to a monumental hangover. When he showed up at the mine office the following day, a letter of termination was on his desk. His drinking buddy of two nights before, who had also missed work but had claimed to be a victim of the twenty-four-hour flu, wouldn't even look him in the eye.

Dad made one telephone call from his desk, asking the operator for time and charges and leaving the correct change in a little pile when he left. The call was to a contractor in Sault Ste. Marie who owed Dad a favour. Dad had saved him months before when the man's on-site bookkeeper had skipped town, leaving a payroll to be made up and cheques to be issued to workers involved in building a plant extension at the Helen Mine.

Dad had stayed up all night, sifting through time cards, payroll records, and whatever else he could get his hands on. By the time the men started filing into the construction shack for their cheques, everything was in order.

The grateful contractor had told Dad then that if he ever needed a job, all he had to do was call. The man was as good as his word, and within a few days we were all packed, the keys to the rented house were returned to the landlord, and we were on our way back to civilization aboard the Algoma Central Railway.

Chapter Twenty-Four
ON TO NEW ADVENTURE

The ACR passenger train taking our family back to Sault Ste. Marie seemed as excited as we were to get going. Black, cinder-laden clouds belched from the engine's smokestack, and steam hissed impatiently from its boiler. At one point, like a skittish stallion pawing at the ground, its wheels spun around with a metallic clatter that made a pack of dogs, cavorting on the station platform, run away howling in terror.

We settled into the green plush seats of one of the coaches. Our mother was trying to restrain baby brother Norm from running up the aisle to visit with other passengers, while Greg and I exchanged excited whispers about what we would do if a gang of train robbers ambushed us somewhere along the way.

Dad was nursing a mild hangover. He'd been able to cut down considerably on his drinking, but his Legion buddies had thrown a surprise farewell party for him the night before and it was obvious a bit of backsliding had occurred.

I don't remember much about the actual train trip, except

ON TO NEW ADVENTURE

that our mother started to get fidgety as we approached
a high trestle over the Magpie River. She was terrified of
heights and had asked the conductor to let her know when
we were getting close to the bridge. When he came by and
said we would be crossing it in a couple of minutes, Maw
walked the length of the coach to the toilet cubicle, where
she locked herself in. Once we had crossed the river, Dad
sent me to knock on the door to tell her it was safe to come
out, much to the annoyed relief of a man who had been waiting to use the facilities.

As when Dad had returned from the war, there was no
brass band to meet us at the station, but my grandfather
Kelly was there with his pickup truck to load our baggage
and drive us to the house that Dad's new boss had found for
us to rent. The various bits and pieces of furniture that my
parents felt were worth saving had come down by freight
train, and Kelly had enlisted the help of a few friends to get
things set up in our new digs. The rest of the contents of our
Wawa house had been given away to friends or carted to the
town dump. A trip to the furniture store replaced what we
had left behind.

There were good times ahead for all of us. Dad's drinking
problem cleared up in due course. Not right away—that only
happens in the movies. But eventually he became a pillar of
the community when he was appointed Clerk of the Small
Claims Court in Sault Ste. Marie. He served two terms as
president of the Ontario Small Claims Court Association
and received accolades from judges, government representa-
tives, and civic officials upon his retirement.

Ironically, one of the highlights of his tenure as head
of the provincial organization was that he was instrumen-
tal in having the Ontario Government bring in a law that
prohibited large corporations from firing workers who had

had their wages garnished three times. While I'm sure he didn't do it as a vendetta against his old employers, it did cause consternation at the Algoma Steel Corporation, whose insensitive executives had used the old three-times-and-you're-out rule to get rid of bothersome employees.

Dad stepped down after his second term as president of the provincial association. The board of directors had been so pleased with his dedication and insight as their chief spokesperson that they offered to waive the rule in their charter that limited a president to two terms of office. Dad was in his mid-sixties at the end of his second term, and he had a great line when he thanked the board of directors at his retirement banquet for their vote of confidence for wanting him to stay on:

"But your constitution won't allow it and my constitution wouldn't take it," he said to gales of laughter and a standing ovation.

Our family over time settled into a routine that included a dog, a car, and summers renting a cottage by the lake. The Beverly Hillbillies became the *Father Knows Best* Andersons.

My parents' long-held desire to have a daughter finally came about. Sister Nancy grew up to become general manager of a hotel in Sault Ste. Marie. Brother Norm got his law degree and was eventually appointed to the bench in the Ontario criminal court system. Brother Greg became a sports reporter for the local paper, then its sports editor— the youngest person up to that time to take the helm of the sports department of a daily newspaper in Canada. Several other milestones in his long career have included ten years as public relations director for the National Hockey League's Vancouver Canucks and sports columnist for the *Vancouver Sun*.

After a brief stint as an elementary school teacher, I too joined the local paper as a general assignment reporter. I leapfrogged my way through several other writing-related jobs to become communications advisor to the federal Minister of Veterans Affairs, travelling the world with him and groups of veterans on pilgrimages to various battle sites. I met so many heroes during that time that I began writing books on Canada's military heritage. I also began going into schools to talk to students about the brave men and women—including my dad—who gave up so much so that we could enjoy the wonderful life that Canada offers.

Every once in a while, a news report from Wawa will catch my eye. And as time softens the images of those long-ago days of the mid to late 1940s, I think back to those wild and sometimes painful years in a town on the brink of frenzy.

Strange as it may seem, I consider myself lucky to have been there.

Epilogue

My dad died four days short of the 44th anniversary of the 1944 Normandy Invasion. My mother had predeceased him by four years and, by the time of his death, there were few of his cronies still left to attend his funeral.

But one of his Royal Canadian Legion comrades, Dick McKinnon, led a colour party of legionnaires who stood ramrod straight near Dad's coffin throughout the service, despite the fact that those four old vets were well into their seventies at the time and that the minister droned on interminably.

Just before they closed the coffin, Dick took an artificial poppy from his lapel and pinned it to my father's Legion blazer. Then the colour party snapped to attention, gave the coffin a smart salute, and marched down the aisle and out of the church. There wasn't a dry eye in the place.

In sifting through Dad's papers a few days after the funeral, I came upon a poem I had written for him many years before, in 1970.

At the time, I had just toured the D-Day beaches in Northern France and had been caught up in a tangle of emotions. Standing on top of an abandoned German gun emplacement, I had gazed down on the coastline where the Allied troops had landed on June 6, 1944.

It was an eerie feeling to know that my father had been one of them and had faced deadly machine gun, rifle, and mortar fire as he and his comrades stormed ashore.

What had really knocked me for a loop was the sudden realization that he had been younger at the time of the Normandy landings than I was during my pilgrimage to the battle site.

Later in the day, I made half a dozen attempts to write him a letter telling him how proud I was of his wartime experiences. Each time, I'd skim over what I had set down, then shake my head at the inadequate words, crumple up the notepaper and start again.

I had just about given up hope of ever getting it right when the opening line of a poem popped into my head. I had never written poetry before—other than some stilted verse I was forced to create for high school English assignments— but the words flowed from my pen as though someone else was dictating them to me. I got the whole thing down in one take and mailed the poem back home without re-reading it, afraid I would discard it as I had the aborted letters.

Dad told me later he had cried when he opened the envelope, mailed from Italy, and had read what I'd written.

In looking over the poem now, I realize it was written at a time when interest in our veterans was waning. I had actually witnessed young people at Remembrance Day ceremonies scoffing at the whole exercise. Happily, some years later along came the movie *Saving Private Ryan* and the television series *Band of Brothers*. And I suppose the passage of time as well had renewed our respect for the sacrifices our veterans had made in both world wars, in Korea, and most recently in Afghanistan.

But the sentiments I expressed in that poem still resonate within me today. In reproducing the words here, I would like to dedicate them to my father and mother, as well as to all the gallant soldiers, male and female, in uniform and in civilian clothes operating behind enemy lines, who sacrificed their lives for our freedom. Some were killed in action; others returned home with physical or emotional scars they would carry for the rest of their lives. But all of them were there to answer the call when the free world needed them.

Medals—such meagre payments for priceless years willingly thrown away—
Are taken from their casual resting place in bureau drawers
And proudly polished to a sheen brass buttons once were given,
Then pinned to coats by hands less steady than when they held a gun.
The faint notes of Reveille can be heard, or are they just imagined
As a final wipe is given to already gleaming shoes.
The dark blue tam is tugged to a familiar cocky angle
And the old soldiers, downing something to ward off November's chill,
Fall in once more.
The ranks are even thinner this year than each had feared.
A different foe—old age—aided perhaps by too many glasses drained
To numb the painful legacy of war,
Has claimed another score or more of comrades,

Bringing home to those remaining the realization that this might be

Their last parade.

No time for that, the pipes and drums have sounded.

It's effort enough to keep in step on a route that lengthens every year.

Nor is it shortened by the knowledge that the crowd of onlookers

Has also thinned.

And some have come to jeer, not pay respects as others did before.

Some of the scoffers, too young to ever have been touched by war,

Snicker when the bugler falters as he plays Taps.

They smirk at each other as the Speaker intones: "Lest we forget."

While two hundred weary eyes regard them sadly

And one hundred hearts whisper: "If you only knew."